"*Cold Hard Truth* is an inspiring, candid, and self-effacing personal insight into what motivates someone to visualize, climb, and endure the most challenging conditions Antarctica's tallest mountain can offer. A gifted storyteller, Len Forkas makes the realities of mountain climbing come to life while simultaneously showing us how his internal quest to help others fuels his achievements. A must-read for anyone aspiring to truly make a difference in climbing, business, or society."

HAP KLOPP
Co-founder and CEO of The North Face
Professor of Innovation at the Hult International Business School
Author of *Conquering The North Face—an Adventure in Leadership*

"Len Forkas takes us up one of the world's most inhospitable mountains, and from the extraordinary experience we appreciate how his lessons from surmounting the extreme should inform our own routines. Thriving on distress, eschewing overconfidence, and honoring the less fortunate helped him reach his summit— and *Cold Hard Truth* well moves us to reach ours too."

MICHAEL USEEM
Faculty Director of the McNulty Leadership Program
Wharton School, University of Pennsylvania
Author of *The Edge: How 10 CEOs Learned to Lead*

"Len Forkas is an adventurer, a businessman and a philanthropist. Each role he fills in his amazing life informs the other. Read this book for a glimpse of all three in action as you also learn a lot about leadership, endurance, and humanity."

STEVE GLADIS, PH.D.
Executive Coach, Team Coach
Author of *Leading Teams: Understanding the Team Leadership Pyramid*

D1290063

"Len's story allows us to imagine ourselves right next to him at every step up the mountain, while describing adventure in a way that translates to the world of business. He teaches us humility, patience, and letting go of what we can't control, reminding us that finding the best in people makes the journey worthwhile."

ALAN D. WHITMAN
CEO of Baker Tilly US

"Len Forkas generously shares the story of his climbing expedition, but the message transcends mountaineering by providing a useful road map for your own journey: Set lofty goals, embrace risk, establish and rely upon a team, and find the grit to reach your target. This is a moving story that will leave you feeling inspired for your own adventures!"

ANDY LEVITT
Founder and CEO of The Purple Carrot

COLD HARD TRUTH

Life Lessons from the
Bottom of the World

LEN FORKAS

HOPECAM
PUBLISHING

Reston, Virginia

Cold Hard Truth: Life Lessons from the Bottom of the World
Copyright © 2022 by Len Forkas

Hopecam Publishing
12100 Sunset Hills Road, Suite C-10
Reston, VA 20190
Hopecam.org

ISBN-13 (paperback): 978-0-9960969-4-2
ISBN-13 (paperback, color interior): 978-0-9960969-7-3
ISBN-13 (hardcover): 978-0-9960969-5-9
ISBN-13 (hardcover, color interior): 978-0-9960969-8-0
ISBN-13 (ebook): 978-0-9960969-6-6

First Edition

Produced in the United States of America

Cover and interior design: Andrew Chapman, Social Motion Publishing

All photos by the author unless otherwise noted.

Cover photo: The author ascending an icy slope on the journey to the summit of Mount Vinson, Antarctica (courtesy of Chris Warner).

Contents

To Elizabeth, Matt, and Viena who have always supported my adventures despite many sleepless nights.

Foreword

The history of Antarctic exploration is an alchemic mixture of exotic settings and colorful characters. Some of them endure, while others die.

Perhaps the best known tale of survival was that of Ernest Shackleton and the crew of the ship *Endurance*, who were trapped by sea ice before even setting foot on the continent. After their ship was crushed by pressure waves, the men climbed onto the floating ice and built shelters from whatever they could salvage. For five-and-a-half months, they lived on the floating ice in makeshift camps. It was only with the breakup of the ice that they could attempt an escape. In a life-or-death gamble, Shackleton and five others sailed an open lifeboat 800 miles across the Southern Ocean, seeking a ship to rescue them. After nearly a month of near misses and improbable odds, Shackleton's team found help. All 28 members of the expedition survived.

A few years earlier, other explorers weren't so lucky. In his 1911–1912 expedition, explorer Robert Falcon Scott not only lost the race to the South Pole by 34 days, he and his four teammates slowly died from exhaustion and starvation while trying to return to their ship. A year later, Douglas Mawson was the sole survivor of a three-month ordeal in which his two partners died (one by falling into a crevasse with the team's food and shelter, the other by a combination of exhaustion and slow poisoning from "husky liver"—a condition known as hypervitaminosis A. The plans of those early expeditions called for eating the huskies and ponies that hauled their gear. From Mawson's diary: "The paws took longest of all to cook, but, treated to lengthy stewing, they became quite digestible."

As a kid, I was captivated by these dreamers, who concocted these misguided adventures and somehow found funding for them. Their books were often poetic: the wind sculpting snow into sastrugi, round rainbows reflecting the rays of the sun shining through a sky full of dancing ice crystals, the black of night that starts one morning and ends one hundred mornings later. The books were also graphic: starvation causing bones to snap and teeth to shatter, the frozen soles of feet peeling away from bone and muscle, blackened fingers and toes auto-amputating with the sound of a snap. Delirium and fevers gripped men for days, only ending when they died in their sleep.

While people still die in Antarctica, babies are also born there (11 at last count). Antarctica, still wild and remote, is now a destination. Cruise ships ply the same coast where Shackleton's team nearly parished. Deep, deep inland, climbers head to the continent's tallest peaks, and skiers slide toward the South Pole (fueled by freeze-dried foods, not husky paws). While Antarctica has become accessible, adventure tourism on the continent is highly controlled and quite expensive. But for those of us infected by Antarctica's history and awed by its beauty, no hurdle is too great.

I'm still buzzing about our trip there. I have been to the top of Everest and taken part in more than 200 international expeditions, but Antarctica and Mount Vinson truly blew my mind. The beauty of the continent is otherworldly. I felt more like I was on a different planet than on a different continent. The 24 hours of light, chaotic swings in temperature, fierce winds, scary crevasses, and rocky summit ridge of Mount Vinson all combined to create the perfect setting for four friends to go on an adventure.

Len will walk you through our team's ups and downs, laying bare our imperfections, mistakes, and near misses. He will remind you that it doesn't take heroism or superhuman powers to climb in Antarctica. What I hope he also teaches you is how to use the same philosophical compass that guided our team: "Don't reach the peak but miss the point." No matter how cold, tired, afraid, or bored we were, we always knew that the point of traveling to the bottom of the world was to learn about the depths of ourselves.

Chris Warner
Aspen, Colorado
November 2021

ANTARCTICA JOURNAL

MOUNT VINSON

ANTARCTIC LOGISTICS EXPEDITIONS

ELEV 16050 FEET

UNION GLACIER
EL 2000 AGL

PUNTA ARENAS
EL 100 AGL

BASE CAMP
EL 7021 AGL

HIGH CAMP
EL 12,402 AGL

LOW CAMP
EL 9121 AGL

LEN FORKAS

DECEMBER 2 - 30, 2018
W/ACHRIS WARNER COMMENTARY

Introduction

This book is about my experience climbing to the summit of Mount Vinson, the tallest mountain in Antarctica. It is one of the "Seven Summits"—the group of mountains made up of the highest peak on each of Earth's continents.

In taking on Mount Vinson, I learned valuable lessons about accepting the unknowable and uncontrollable situations of high-altitude mountaineering, an adventure I documented each day by filling my journal with colorful sketches, diagrams, and observations. When I was an architecture student at Ball State University, my professors required me to carry a sketchbook on every road trip or school excursion to document my surroundings. As a father traveling with young children, I rediscovered the joy of sketching on our family vacations. The habit stuck.

Every day climbing the mountain was specifically dedicated to a child fighting cancer who had been supported by Hopecam, a nonprofit I had founded in 2002 after my own son was diagnosed with leukemia. Hopecam connects homebound children to friends at school using webcam technology and tablet computers, a need we have all come to understand since COVID-19. The struggles I faced on the mountain are nothing compared to their everyday ordeals.

On this expedition, we made plenty of mistakes. Some of my

own errors put myself and others in danger. But we learned valuable lessons from every mistake, forgave one another, and we moved on. As a team, we honored each other's roles and placed our trust in one another while confronting uncontrollable challenges that brought, in turns, joy, fear, and dread. The leadership lessons I gained came from sharing the company of the right people with the right skills, solving problems, listening carefully, and working as a team toward a simple common goal: Summit the mountain, have fun doing it, and, most importantly, come home safely.

Prologue

Despite so many delays and frustrating postponements, we could now see the summit. Months of planning and preparation had led to this moment, this opportunity. Only a few hundred feet above us loomed the peak of Mount Vinson, the tallest mountain in Antarctica and one of the fabled "Seven Summits" of the world.

Yet, too soon our time began to run short again. Once more, the icy winds picked up in velocity and the subzero temperatures plunged further—now well below zero. The four of us clipped into the steel pickets leading along the final stretch to the top and hurried, as best we could under such extreme conditions, to complete the final stretch upward before it was indeed too late.

Training on the Mount Baker, Washington, glacier
Here I am, climbing the ropes up a sheer wall of ice in a crevasse 50 feet deep.
(Photo courtesy of Lyra Pierotly.)

CHAPTER ONE
AUGUST 2018

"Many have the will to win,
but few have the will to prepare to win."
Fielding H. Yost, head coach, University of Michigan, 1901–1923

IN AUGUST 2018, I RECEIVED an unusual email message from my friend Chris Warner. "Hey Len, I am climbing Mt. Vinson with some friends. Do you want to join us?"

Chris was the founder and CEO of the Earth Treks chain of climbing gyms, which he grew into a national presence until selling it to a private equity company. An accomplished mountaineer, he has successfully guided more than 200 expeditions to many of the most challenging peaks on Earth. He is a veteran climber of Mount Everest and K2, the world's two tallest mountains, as well as many of the other 26,000-foot peaks of the Himalayas.

Mount Vinson would present an entirely different adventure, a challenge even for a seasoned mountaineer like Chris. Formally known as Vinson Massif, it is the highest peak in Antarctica—a remote quartzite pinnacle overlooking the most forbidding continent in the world. Rising 16,050 feet above the Ronne Ice Shelf, Vinson stands 750 miles from the South Pole amid the Ellsworth

Mountains, with a steep ascent marked by flowing glaciers and deep crevasses. Temperatures can plunge beyond 40 degrees below zero, the frigid point at which the Fahrenheit and Celsius scales converge.

The only high peak I had ever summited was Kilimanjaro, and that was five years earlier. Kilimanjaro practically straddles the equator, as far from Earth's poles as you can get. A 19,341-foot peak towering over Tanzania, it was a challenging ascent, but it required little in the way of technical climbing that Vinson would surely call for. Chris had already assembled a capable duo to climb with him. He asked me to be the team's fourth and final member. It was too tantalizing an invitation to ignore. I picked up my phone and called him.

"Why on earth would you want a novice like me to join your team for Vinson?" I asked. "I don't know shit about climbing."

Chris dismissed my inexperience. "It's more important who you climb with than where you climb," he said. "Besides, we need a mule."

Now I understood. Chris was planning a fully self-supported expedition. Antarctica had no porters to heave mountaineers' gear up the mountains. We would have to carry ours by ourselves, without even the support enjoyed by the mountain's other teams. They ran multiple expeditions throughout the season, with plenty of supplies in place along the route. We would have none of that. Chris's other two teammates were experienced, but they were not young men anymore.

Mike Paterson, an emergency room doctor in Evergreen, Colorado, was a rugged outdoorsman and a dedicated philanthropist. Like me, he had climbed Kilimanjaro, as well as Denali in Alaska and Aconcagua in Argentina. Each of these was among the Seven Summits—the tallest peaks on each of the world's seven continents. If we were successful, Vinson would be his fourth of the seven. Mike was up to the task. He had led wilderness rafting trips, volunteered at Ebola clinics in Africa, and taught surgery in Haiti. But he was nearly 60 years old and was nursing a debilitating ankle injury that would make descending the mountain an even greater challenge.

Guntis Brands was a retired entrepreneur and co-founder of Glacier Holdings, a venture capital firm. Guntis was born in Latvia, but after making a fortune in the wood kiln business, he settled in the adventure outpost of Zermatt, Switzerland, where he lived on a mountaintop near the famous Matterhorn. Climbing was part of his DNA, and his experience as a mountaineer was impressive. Guntis had summited five Himalayan peaks topping 26,000 feet and many other smaller peaks. But he was 67 and not as strong as he used to be. Even Chris, who was five years younger than me, was feeling the tug of age.

At 59, I was no spring chicken, either. But Chris knew that, while I was not a mountaineer, I was in top shape and knew a little something about physically demanding challenges and adventures that border upon the impossible. Chris and I first met in Golden, Colorado, in 2014, when I was writing *What Spins the Wheel*. The book chronicled the 11 days I had spent competing in the Race Across America—a 3,000-mile cycling competition that pushed riders to their limits as they pedaled from Oceanside, California, to Annapolis, Maryland. Powering yourself coast to coast on two wheels was a test of the tallest order, but putting the ordeal on paper was also proving a challenge. Back then, I knew Chris only by reputation, but I was sure he could help guide me. In addition to our shared passion for endurance sports, Chris was a success-ful businessman, an Emmy Award nominee for his documentary work, and a published author.

We hit it off. The two of us had a lot in common, we discov-

ered. We were both Catholic school boys from middle-class families. We went to college, earned degrees, and became successful
businessmen with a love for adventure. Over eggs and coffee, we
discovered that we had both registered to race later that year in the
Leadville 100 mountain bike race, a quad-burning course through
the Colorado high country beginning and ending in the mountain
town of Leadville. The night before the race, we met again over
pizza in Vail. Chris's wife, Melinda, was providing water and food
for Chris on the Leadville course, and she offered to do the same for
me. Chris and I both finished the race in 10 hours—no small feat. I
had signed up for the Leadman Series, which brought me back to
Colorado a week later for a 100-mile running race. Chris joined my
support crew and helped me cross the finish line in 29 hours and 30
minutes, earning me the coveted "Leadman" title.

Chris also knew I had Vinson in my sights. Adventurers around
the world aspire to climb the Seven Summits. After scaling Kilimanjaro with my son, Matt, I longed to see the top of the other six. For
most who try, Vinson is the last they will attempt. It is the remotest
of them all, far more isolated than Mount Everest, and it endures
some of the most inhospitable weather on the planet. Frigid and
desolate, Antarctica is an ice desert. It supports no life at all, except
for lichen near the sea. Penguins and sea lions inhabit the coastline,
but they have to dive into the ocean to find food. Even bacteria
can't survive past a few miles from the coast. Yet it was here that I
longed to go, to climb its highest and most forbidding peak.

I had another reason to venture to Antarctica—a more personal
one. After I ran my first marathon, I swore I'd never put myself
through the torture again. But when Matt was diagnosed with leukemia at nine years old, I turned to exercise to deal with the stress.
I started running and cycling longer and longer distances. I signed

up for triathlons, then marathons, then ultramarathons. During that transformation, I became driven by endurance sports. They became a part of my makeup and my approach to the world.

These competitions fed another passion of mine. In 2003, I started a nonprofit I called Hopecam. Its purpose is to help children with cancer connect with classmates when their treatment keeps them away from school. Hopecam does this by supplying and deploying webcams and tablet computers. In the wake of COVID-19 lockdowns, this approach has become commonplace, but in 2003 it was a real challenge. Matt's isolation had been devastating for him, but being able to interact with his classmates turned his life around. I wanted to give other kids with cancer the same chance he had. When I raced, sponsors contributed to my efforts per mile, raising thousands of dollars for my new organization. When we partnered with world-renowned St. Jude Children's Research Hospital after completing Race Across America, I was able to build Hopecam from a local charity into a nonprofit with a national scope.

Originally, Chris and I had planned to race mountain bikes across Mongolia together. But when he couldn't make it to Mongolia he invited me to join his team in Antarctica. I was pumped. There I envisioned that I could both tackle one of the Seven Summits and knock off a marathon, too—even if I had to run the 26.2 miles by myself. That's another goal of mine: To run a marathon on each continent. Yes, I believe in dreaming big. My mantra has been "go big or go home."

If anybody had the skills and wisdom to get the team up and down Vinson Massif safely, I knew it was Chris. And Chris knew I had the muscle and drive to make the journey with him. I wasn't a whiner. I wasn't a quitter.

Within a few days of agreeing, however, I realized what I had gotten myself into. We would attempt Vinson in December, giving me only a few months to train and acquire the skills for what would be the most ambitious expedition of my life. But the timing was necessary. It would be the height of the Antarctic summer, when the temperatures would be at their highest (though still well below freezing) and the sun would circle the sky without ever dipping below the horizon. We were traveling to a land and season of perpetual daylight.

How do you prepare in such a short time to climb icy slopes and traverse crevasse fields in subzero temperatures under the weight of a heavy pack, slogging along with bulky boots, crampons, and an ice axe? Honestly, I had no idea, But I knew that Mark Gunglonson did. Mark was the CEO of Mountain Madness, the Seattle-based mountaineering outfitter that supported the Kilimanjaro climb I had completed with my son. When I told Mark what I was embarking on, he arranged for a private training session on Mount Baker, a 10,781-foot volcano in Washington state. For three rainy days, mountain guide Lyra Pierotly was assigned to teach me how to move about on the ice. Within the climbing community, Lyra was known as the glacier queen. Having led expeditions to challenging, technical peaks such as Mount Rainier, Denali, and Elbrus, she was an expert at glacier mountaineering.

Mike Paterson, the emergency room surgeon who would soon be my teammate on Mount Vinson, would join me in this training. Mike already knew the techniques and the gear, but they were new to me. Lyra taught me how to use an ice axe to stop a fall on a glacier. Crampons, she explained, would help hold my feet to the icy slope. Looking like vintage roller skates without the key, they were soles with metallic teeth, that clamp onto the bottom of climbers' boots. A climbing harness, wrapped around my waist and thighs, would secure me to the rope I would rely on. A jumar, a gearing system that locks when it's weighted and unlocks when it isn't, would function as a brake in case of a fall while ascending fixed ropes. Lyra even had a rescue plan in case we plummeted into a deep crevasse at the bottom of the world. For that worst-case scenario, we had to place our trust in a simple Prusik knot. It's a short section of rope knotted around the climbing rope. It could save our lives. What we needed to do, in case of such an emergency, was loosen the knot and pull up. Next, Lyra told us, let the knot tighten. Then loosen it and pull up again. From there, we had to let it tighten once more. Repeat that procedure enough times, she said, and we'd be on solid ground again.

It sounds simple enough, doesn't it? But in those first few days on Mount Baker, overlooking the North Cascade mountains as the heavens rained more "liquid sunshine" down upon us, I wondered what I had gotten myself into. I felt like a hockey player who couldn't skate, sent out to face off against Wayne Gretzky or Alex Ovechkin. How could I expect to climb the highest peak at the base of the world when I was scrambling to stay on two feet? But there's something to be said about learning from a quality teacher. Somehow, in just a few days, Lyra had me feeling about as comfortable as I could while hanging on a rope off a cliff.

It soon became apparent, though, that mountaineering skills wouldn't be enough. I would need strength training very different from anything I had attempted before. Climbing would use muscles I never had to rely on in running or cycling, and I didn't have much time to develop them. I hadn't set foot in a gym in seven years, when I traded in my gym membership for a fitness room in my basement.

I signed up at Parable Training, in Chantilly, Virginia, not far from my home. Owner Katie Hanger subjected me to dragging sleds, donning a 40-pound vest for pull-ups, and squatting with kettle bells. The exercises made my upper body and quads scream, but within weeks I began to see real results. I could sit up straighter. I could lift and ascend with a 60-pound pack without tipping over. I felt as prepared as possible, albeit in the comfort of suburban Virginia, to haul supplies up the slopes of Mount Vinson.

My next adventure may surprise some of you. It was shopping. Pricey mountaineering brands became household names as I put my credit card limit to the test. My shopping list included 75 items, all of which had to be up to the challenges of Antarctica's rugged mountains and frigid temperatures. Triple-layer climbing boots. A down-feathered sleeping bag for minus-40-degree nights. A jacket that made me look like the Michelin man. Since I would be hauling my own gear, everything would also have to be as light as possible.

One week before my departure, I made a final foray to acclimate myself to high altitudes. Chris paired me with Jeff Mascaro, an experienced Earth Treks trainer and mountain guide. Jeff led me on two acclimatization ascents at the base of Loveland Pass, along Colorado's Continental Divide. November had brought winter temperatures to the Colorado high country. With the thermometer registering in the 20s Fahrenheit and winds blowing at 40 miles per hour, we climbed five hours to the summit of Grizzly Peak, at an elevation of 13,425 feet. This was all the training that time would permit. On December 1, 2018, I loaded two 50-pound bags into the trunk of a taxi and headed to Dulles International Airport. My itinerary would take me from Washington, D.C., to Houston, Texas, from Houston to Chile, from Chile to Antarctica. The plan was to return on December 20, well in time to spend Christmas with my family. It was a cherished holiday for us. I didn't want to miss it, so the five-day buffer would allow for the unpredictability of Antarctica. When explorer Ernest Shackleton sailed the *Endurance* to the continent in 1914, his crew became stranded in a 16-month ordeal. Times had changed, though. For us not to make it back in time for Christmas, something would really have to go wrong.

Lesson 1: Prepare for the job.

Ancient Greek poet Archilochus wrote: "We don't rise to the level of our expectations; we fall to the level of our training." Success comes from knowing you did your best to become the best you can become. Not wanting to let down my teammates, I dedicated time to learning new skills, practiced in the field, underwent strength training, and invested in the gear and tools I would need to be successful.

DAY = -3

▪ LOGISTICS ▪

GUNTIS, MICHAEL & CHRIS ALL
ARRIVED SAFELY AND OUR BREAKFAST
WE MAPPED OUT THE SCHEDULE & SUPPLY
LIST OF PROVISIONS WE WOULD NEED FOR
THE EXPEDITION.

SCHEDULE	GROCERIES
DAY 1: UNION GLACIER	· PANCAKE MIX
DAY 2: VINSON BASE	· DINNER ROLLS
DAY 3: VINSON BASE	· INSTANT OATMEAL
DAY 4: LOW CAMP.	· SOUP MIX
DAY 5: CARRY HIGH CAMP	· POWDERED MILK
DAY 6: HIGH CAMP	· HONEY.
DAY 7: REST DAY.	· COFFEE + TEA.
DAY 8: VINSON SUMMIT	· CHEESE
DAY 9: SHINN SUMMIT	· HAMBURGERS
DAY 10: VINSON BASE	· CONDIMENTS
DAY 11: UNION GLACIER	· TRASH BAGS
DAY 12: PUNTA ARENAS	· RAISINS
	· JAM. BUTTER
	· SANITISER

THIS WOULD ALLOW FOR A
RETURN TO PUQ ON DEC 18th.
AND A 3 DAY WEATHER BUFFER

CHAPTER TWO
DECEMBER 5

"Start where you are. Use what you have. Do what you can."
Arthur Ashe, celebrated professional tennis player

FOUR DAYS LATER, THE ADVENTURE began to unfold. My three teammates and I had arrived separately in Punta Arenas, Chile, where we checked into the Hotel Rey Don Felipe, a three-story business hotel in the heart of the city, two blocks from the Plaza de Armas. Positioned near the southernmost tip of South America, Punta Arenas serves as the jump-off point for adventures into the Patagonia wilderness and excursions across the Drake Passage to Antarctica. This small city would be our last taste of luxury before our expedition began.

Over breakfast in front of the fireplace in the hotel's stone-and-timber lobby, we spread out our maps and gear checklists. I hadn't seen Chris since that Leadville race in Colorado four years earlier. He was as I remembered him: Tall and silver-haired, with a trimmed beard, a hearty sense of humor, and a commanding presence.

It was great to reunite with Mike Paterson after our shared training experience in Washington. He was looking lean and fit, with white hair and a short mustache. While that ankle injury was still dogging him, he planned to power through it, and from the time I had spent training with him, I had no doubt he could. Mike had a headstrong demeanor honed in the life-or-death urgency of the emergency room. If anyone could summit Antarctica's tallest peak with an injured ankle, it was Mike.

This was the first I had met Guntis Brands, and from the moment we exchanged greetings, he won me over with his calm presence. Guntis seemed like Mike's opposite. When he spoke, it was carefully and deliberately. He shared thoughtful observations about climbing, teamwork, and life, always in hushed tones. Guntis was slim and weathered, with an impish smile and a shock of wild, sandy hair. I sensed that the man from the mountaintop in Switzerland would be our sage, and a calming influence on the team.

Chris laid out our adventure before us. The next day, we would fly for four hours to Union Glacier Camp, 600 miles from the South Pole. The camp wouldn't be anything fancy, but compared to the rest of the continent, it would be luxury—showers, toilets, fresh-cooked meals, and Chilean beer. It would also be busy. Union Glacier Camp served as the staging area for most Antarctic adventures. Climbers, skiers, and penguin watchers all gathered there before setting off in different directions on their itineraries.

From there, we would take a ski plane on a short hop to the Mount Vinson Base Camp, where our ascent would begin. Our time on the mountain would be about 10 days, if the weather cooperated, making use of two established camps set up on the massif. From Base Camp, we would face a 5.6-mile haul up 2,100 feet along the Branscomb Glacier to reach Low Camp, at an elevation of about 9,000 feet. The route would be gradual enough to allow us to drag 70 pounds of gear on sleds behind us, but our journey would be riddled with crevasses that could be deadly if we stumbled in. We would rope together, so if one of us went over the edge, or a sled tumbled in, the rest of us could arrest the fall. At least that was the plan.

The approach to High Camp would take us up the headwall, a long climb with a 40-degree pitch—like a stairway without the stairs. Instead, we would dig in with crampons and ice axes and clip into a series of fixed ropes. If we fell, we would rely on the jumars to stop us. From High Camp, at 12,402 feet, our summit bid would take us up a steep slope to Vinson's rocky ridgeline, which would lead us to the top of the bottom of the planet. Then, it would be a daylong journey back to Base Camp.

But before departing for Antarctica, since this expedition was self-supporting, we needed to do some grocery shopping. The four of us headed to the local Unimarc store to stock up on provisions. When we finished, we loaded a taxi with 100 pounds of supplies—enough to keep us alive for 21 days—far more time than we should need. Chicken. Pasta. Bread. Lunchmeat. Canned goods. Oatmeal. Powdered milk. Sugar. Toilet paper. Honey. Granola. Chocolate. Coffee.

"¡Eso es mucha comida! ¿Adónde vas?" asked the taxi driver. We attempted to explain our journey in broken Spanish.

That evening, Chris schooled us on what may have been our most important gear on the mountain: the liquid gas stoves that would heat our water and cook our food, and the tents that would shelter us. Both could be tricky to operate or set up, he warned. The stoves were light and effective—standard issue for mountaineers—but they could be temperamental. They required a measured, thoughtful approach that could be challenging on the side of a frozen mountain with gale-force winds blowing. The stoves used small tanks of liquid gas—miniature versions of a backyard grill—and they had to be started carefully to properly ignite the burner. If not primed with the right amount of fuel, they could erupt in a

AFTER GROCERY SHOPPING WE WERE
GIVEN AN ORIENTATION OF OUR TWO
CRITICAL GEAR-TOOLS-THAT OUR
SURVIVAL WILL DEPEND ON, ON THE
MOUNTAIN.

STOVE & TENTS.

THE STOVE WORKS
USING LIQUID
PROPANE THAT
WILL BE PROVIDED
AT VINSON BASE
CAMP. CHRIS
HELPED EXPLAIN THE SETUP - OPERATIONAL
AND SAFETY TIPS WHEN OPERATING
THE STOVE. THE TENT WAS SET UP
IN FRONT OF THE HOTEL IN THE
WIND - GREAT ... SIMPLE ... FAST TENTS

(2) PERSON TENT
SIERRA DESIGNS "METEOR"
IS THE TENT NAME &
MANUFACTURER.

MSR
DRAGONFLY
STOVE

gas.

MSR

fireball. We would carry two stoves, Chris said, in case one failed. If both shut down, the trip was over. Without heat, there is no water in Antarctica. Without water, there would be no food.

Assembling the two-person tents seemed straightforward enough on the hotel's grassy lawn. But what about on the ice, in subzero temperatures, amid howling winds, after an exhausting day of climbing? The tents were rugged, but one slip of a carbon fiber tentpole could slice open the yellow-and-blue nylon dome. These delicate items would keep us alive on Mount Vinson. We would have to be careful with them.

Next to Chris, Mike, and Guntis, I felt self-conscious about my lack of experience with these basic mountaineering staples. After our group split up, I practiced setting up and breaking down the tents a few more times myself. This was a basic part of our expedition I didn't want to screw up.

As the sun rose the next day, the waiting game began. We hoped to fly the following day, Friday, but that depended on the weather— and so far, this expedition season in Antarctica had been challenging. The first teams to reach the continent set up camp in 25-knot winds with the mercury at minus-25 degrees Fahrenheit. Planes would not even depart if conditions were not favorable at both Punta Arenas and the Union Glacier landing strip in Antarctica. Our bags were loaded. We waited. On Friday morning, gale-force winds pummeled both ends of the flight path. By evening, they still hadn't let up. We soon learned to embrace such uncertainty.

As I waited, I took to the coastline for short runs, enjoying my last moments in the temperate world. Low hills fell off into a rocky shore along the Straits of Magellan. To the south, 1,186 miles away, lay my destination. I would be there soon, if the winds ever let up.

On Saturday morning, they unexpectedly did. After a 6 a.m.

THURSDAY DECEMBER 6, 2018
PUNTA ARENAS, CHILE

THIS IS MY 3RD. DAY IN
PUNTA ARENAS AND IN
TWO DAYS WE WILL BE IN TRANSIT
TO ANTARCTICA ABOARD THE
ILYUSIAN FOUR ENGINE JET

OUR TEAM IS NOW PREPARING OUR CHECK LISTS
OF GEAR, FOOD, PROVISIONS ETC FOR THE
UPCOMING EXPEDITION. WE SPENT THE
AFTERNOON PACKING AND WEIGHING ALL OF OUR
GEAR TO MAKE SURE WE DID NOT EXCEED THE

208 KILOGRAMS
457 LBS OF GEAR

PLUS OUR CARRY-ON LUGGAGE WHICH
HAD TO BE SMALL ENOUGH TO FIT UNDER THE
SEAT IN FRONT OF YOU.

IN THE AFTERNOON I RAN FOR 3.3 MILES IN THE
CITY ALL THROUGHOUT THE NEIGHBORHOODS.

wakeup call, our team was on the jetway at Presidente Carlos Ibáñez del Campo International Airport. When I competed in Race Across America, I dedicated each leg of the journey to a child Hopecam supported. I wanted to do the same on this adventure. Standing near the jetway, we dedicated our departure day to a 16-year-old girl from Scotts Bluff, Nebraska, named Sofia. Born on New Year's Day, Sofia was diagnosed with a rare form of brain cancer called anaplastic astrocytoma. I knew the struggles she and the other Hopecam kids go through are far worse than the harshest weather or steepest climb we expected to encounter on Vinson.

We videotaped a dedication to Sofia and uploaded it to the Hopecam Facebook page. It would be our last chance to post a photo or video until our return. In Antarctica, our communications would be limited to satellite phones and radios, including a device Chris carried that could send text messages by satellite from his iPhone to family and friends.

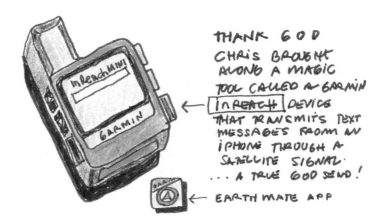

THANK GOD CHRIS BROUGHT ALONG A MAGIC TOOL CALLED A GARMIN InREACH DEVICE THAT TRANSMITS TEXT MESSAGES FROM AN iPHONE THROUGH A SATELLITE SIGNAL. ...A TRUE GOD SEND!

← EARTH MATE APP

Awaiting us on the runway was the plane that would carry us four and a half hours across the Drake Passage. It was a four-engine Ilyushin Il-76, a stocky Russian transport jet whose reputa-

FRIDAY DECEMBER 7th 2018
PUNTA ARENAS, CHILE

FLIGHT DAY TODAY WAS CANCELLED DUE TO WEATHER AT UNION GLACIER ☹

I WENT FOR A RUN ALONG THE WATERFRONT FOR 3.5 MI AND SPENT SOME TIME AT THE HOTEL GYM WITH WEIGHTS AND SOME CORE EXERCISES

LUNCH WAS IN TOWN WITH CHRIS, MIKE AND GUNTIS AT A LOCAL PLACE CALLED LA LUNA — FUN PLACE

DECORATED WITH POST CARDS & LETTERS PASTED ON THE WALLS AND CEILINGS

WE WAITED FOR THE ALE TEAM TO CALL WITH A STATUS REPORT ON THE ILYUSIAN FLIGHT. THE PICKED UP OUR BAGS THURSDAY NIGHT.

THE DAY ENDED WITH DINNER IN TOWN AND LOTS OF ANTICIPATION FOR A FLIGHT ON SATURDAY MORNING.

tion as a military workhorse in forbidding climates made it one of the only jets in the world that can land safely on Union Glacier Camp's blue ice runway.

A five-person Ukrainian team commanded the aircraft. One technician guarding the hatch looked like the bald, musclebound character Drax from the movie *Guardians of the Galaxy*. The crew members were all former Russian military, and they meant business. As I stepped aboard, I saw that only the forward section of the plane was outfitted with seats—eight rows, three on each side—to accommodate our team and others heading to Antarctica. Sunlight streamed through just two small round windows in the entry doors. Above us stretched bundles of wires, cables, netting, and insulation. We would not see our flight across the passage firsthand. Instead, a large flat-panel TV mounted above the cockpit door would broadcast video of the view from the pilots' windshield.

The Ilyushin roared off the runway. The engine sound inside the cabin was so deafening it rendered my noise-cancelling headphones useless. In front of us, the monitor showed the narrow strip of Patagonia disappear into blue sky. Once airborne, the view from the camera was replaced with documentaries about Antarctica—a crash course on a continent I knew so little about. While most of the passengers slept to the droning hum of the jet engines, I was wide awake in self-doubt, regretting my decision to join Chris. I had no business being on this trip. I felt like a Single-A baseball player being called up to the Major League. A novice expected to perform like a veteran. Like an infantryman marching into battle for the first time, I would have to face the fear of the unknown, figure it out and adapt. But though it might seem like the weather in Antarctica would be trying to kill me, at least no one would be shooting at me. An hour before landing, the pilot's voice crackled over the loud-

Day Zero

SATURDAY DECEMBER 8th.
PUNTA ARENAS TO UNION GLACIER

FINALLY THE WAKE UP CALL CAME FOR AN
8:00 AM PICKUP FOR OUR FLIGHT TO THE ICE.
GATE 1 AT THE MAIN AIRPORT.
THE 4 1/2 HOUR FLIGHT OPERATED BY RUSSIAN
PILOTS LANDS ON THE ICE AT UNION GLACIER

WE LANDED WITHOUT INCIDENT AT
3:30 PAM AND AFTER A QUICK 15 MIN
SHUTTLE WE ARRIVED AT GLACIER CAMP.

speaker. To help us adapt to conditions at Union Glacier, he said, he would be lowering the cabin temperature to freezing.

From our backpacks, we pulled layers of fleece and down and prepared for this next, icy chapter of our lives. As we buckled in for landing, the documentaries disappeared, replaced by the pilots' view. The vast whiteness of Antarctica filled the windscreen. At the center, a blue ice runway wheeled in front of us, looming larger and larger. Soon, the plane touched down gently upon this surreal terrain, but the following noise became deafening. For two minutes, we covered our ears as the engines roared and fought the smoothness of the ice. Brakes were useless, I realized. To land on a glacier, the plane needed full reverse thrust to stop. We had arrived.

Vans fitted with cat tracks met us at the landing strip and hauled us four miles to camp. There we found a small city of adventurers awaiting us. It was nowhere near as crowded as I had heard Mount Everest Base Camp to be, but we were hardly alone. In addition to all the other Antarctic adventurers, 33 other climbers from five other teams from around the globe were aiming to summit Mount Vinson during the same time frame. Amid dozens of clam-shell tents laid out in even rows, we pitched our own nylon tents and met up in the mess hall for an early dinner. Our adventure was about to begin.

Lesson 2: We grow most when we are uncomfortable.

Purposefully placing myself in an awkward spot, accepting uncertainty and allowing myself to be vulnerable opened the gateway to personal growth. The definition of "adventure" is being part of an unusual, exciting, and usually risky experience with an uncertain outcome. Our adventure was underway, and it was both frightening and exciting in equal measure.

...SINCE THE CONTINENT OF ANTARCTICA HAS NO POPULATION IT HAS NEVER HAD ANY GOVERNMENT RULES OF LAW.

STAMPS BELOW AND ABOVE AT THE ALÉ TENT FOR BOTH THE UNION GLACIER AND MT VINSON. VERY NICE RETRO DESIGN ON THIS ONE

MANY PEOPLE WERE STAMPING THEIR PASSPORTS AND SOME CHINESE CLIMBERS WERE STAMPING LONG PAPER SCROLLS THAT LOOKED LIKE JOURNALS... THEY ASKED FOR MANY OF THE GUESTS TO AUTOGRAPH THE SCROLLS AND WRITE COMMENTS ON THE PARCHMONT PAPER

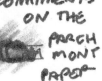

CHAPTER THREE
DECEMBER 9

"Incompetence is certainty in the absence of expertise.
Overconfidence is certainty in the presence of expertise."
Malcolm Gladwell, bestselling nonfiction author

UNION GLACIER CAMP SITS about 600 miles from the South Pole at the base of the Ellsworth Mountains, a rugged range stretching for 217 miles along the western edge of the Ronne Ice Shelf. Its Quonset hut served as the heart of Antarctic civilization, a place where adventurers gathered as they set off and returned from their expeditions. The dining hall filled with tales as climbers returned from Vinson, or like us, prepared to set off. It felt like the scene in *Star Wars* when Luke Skywalker enters a cantina filled with characters from other galaxies. Italian adventurer Danilo Callegari was readying to climb the mountain and parachute from the summit. Chinese ecotourists were preparing to visit emperor penguins at Gould Bay. The staff hailed from the United Kingdom, Chile, Denmark, Nepal, and the United States. As we settled in, we followed updates from American adventurer Colin O'Brady and British adventurer Louis Rudd as they raced each other to complete the first unsupported expedition across the continent via the South Pole.

SUNDAY DECEMBER 9th.
UNION GLACIER. 2,100 ELEV.

THE DINING HUT IS WHERE WE SPEND MOST OF MONDAY WAITING TO HEAR FROM FLIGHT CONTROL THE TIMES THE TWIN ENGINE OTTER WILL DEPART TO VINSON BASE CAMP. AT NOON BOTH PLANES DEPARTED - WITH 8 PEOPLE IN EACH PLANE. AT 3:00 P.M. THEY RETURNED AND DEPARTED AT 3:30 P.M. SHUTTLING ANOTHER 8

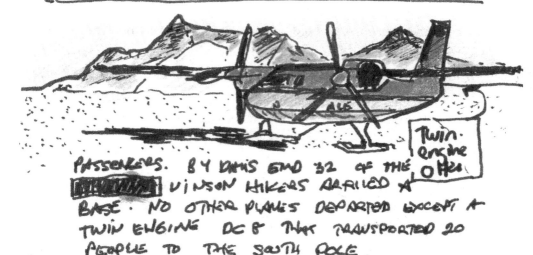

Twin engine Otter

PASSENGERS. BY THIS END 32 OF THE ████████ VINSON HIKERS ARRIVED A BASE. NO OTHER PLANES DEPARTED EXCEPT A TWIN ENGINE DC 8 THAT TRANSPORTED 20 PEOPLE TO THE SOUTH POLE.

Our team was not out to break any world records. At the time, we just wanted to catch a ride on a twin-engine prop plane for a 45-minute flight to Mount Vinson Base Camp. But there were 37 climbers hoping to reach the peak, and just two small planes to ferry us all there. We had hoped to reach Base Camp the previous night, but Union Glacier had a pecking order, and we were at the bottom. Our four-person team would be on the last flight out. With heavy clouds and 30-knot winds at Base Camp, it was hard to say when that would be.

Despite clear skies here, our flight would have to wait again. Biding our time at Union Glacier was hardly painful. Mike and I borrowed fat-tire bikes from the camp and pedaled out to the runway, passing a six-foot-tall plywood cutout Christmas tree along the way. It reminded us that the holidays were only weeks away and that the clock was ticking if we hoped to make it home in time. Chris pulled out his device to text our families back home. His first entry conveyed both patience and hope:

> **Union Glacier Camp, 12-9-2018**
> Poor weather resulted in only 3 of the 6 flights to Vinson Base Camp today. We are forced to spend an extra night at the Union Glacier camp. Hard to complain with hot showers, catered food and entertainment. Temps are -8c but with the strength of the sun it feels balmy. Fingers are crossed that we fly in the morning. Team is still happy. (Chris Warner)

The day felt surprisingly warm, despite the actual temperature only reaching 10 degrees. Antarctica's dry climate could make even frigid temperatures bearable, and the solar radiation reflecting off the white snow warmed our bodies. December brings Antarctica the most sun of any place on the planet. Although the continent is covered in ice, in terms of precipitation, it is the driest place on Earth. Fewer than six inches of snow fall on Antarctica most years. Some parts receive no snow at all. With temperatures never cresting the freezing point, even days of 24 hours of sunlight cause little melting.

While we waited, we got to know our fellow climbers—six teams representing 19 different countries. The largest, led by expert guide Mike Hamill, was a group of 12 whose goal was expressed by the team's name: Climbing the Seven Summits. Antarctic Logistics and Expeditions (ALE), the company that operated the camps, had a nine-person team. The Amical team from Germany had five. Argentinian Tomas Ceppi led Mountain Professionals, an international team of four women climbers. New Zealander Andy Cole led Adventure Consultants, a team of three. In all likelihood, Mount Vinson was part of the Seven Summits plan for some of them, too.

Climbing Kilimanjaro had taught me to enjoy this camaraderie with a like-minded group of adventurers, but the exchanges weren't always pleasant. "Use your head, mate," a voice beside me said as I filled my water bottles at the mess hall. It was Andy Cole, from Adventure Consultants, who took it upon himself to scold me for planning to haul four one-liter bottles onto a cramped plane. "You don't take extra weight on the plane. Melt some water at Base Camp," he said.

I shrugged him off, but he seemed determined to get my goat. The direct sun let us lounge outside the mess hall. I set up four lawn chairs from a storage locker and arranged them with a view toward the runway so our team could sit together. After ducking into the latrine, I returned to find Andy sitting comfortably in my chair, chatting up my teammates. Avoiding confrontation, I returned with another chair and held my tongue. Andy was indeed knowledgeable—an experienced guide and a former military mountaineer for the New Zealand Army Adventure Training Centre, where his work included training special forces personnel—but he came off as a know-it-all. I wasn't anxious to create conflict on our expedition, but I didn't look forward to sharing Mount Vinson with him, even if we weren't on the same climbing team.

Exchanges with other climbers were far more pleasant, however, and we passed the time playing game after game of cornhole until we got the word we could take off. The twin-engine Otter, fitted with skis over the landing gear, was ready. Four of the 10 seats in its cramped fuselage were reserved for us. We packed about two dozen mountaineering duffel bags in the cargo hold behind the cockpit and strapped them down with heavy netting. Soon, the aircraft lifted off, and we headed west toward Mount Vinson Base Camp.

Antarctica may be the most extreme environment in the world, and so it attracts some of the most daring and skilled pilots and air transit companies around. Founded in 1955, Calgary-based Ken Borek Air operated the largest fleet of turbo-prop planes that serviced some of the most remote places on the planet. Its pilots were legendary for their daring rescues in Antarctica and across the globe. They had 35 years of experience flying the de Havilland DHC-6, a plane renowned for its ability to take off and land on extremely short runways. Its reliability, maneuverability, and versatility made it ideal to reach the remote Base Camp.

Peering out the window from 3,500 feet, I understood why these pilots refused to fly in anything less than perfect conditions. Below us lay nothing but mountains, glaciers, and crevasse fields. If we had an emergency, the rugged landscape offered no safe place to land. Rescue would be all but impossible. Union Glacier had no helicopter and returning on foot across these crevasses would be

Day 2
• UNION GLACIER •
• DECEMBER 10th •

WAITING FOR THE (2)
THIRD DAY AT UNION
GLACIER FOR THE
WEATHER TO CLEAR AT
BASE CAMP FOR OUR
DEPARTURE.

THE GROUP THAT IS COORDINATING OUR TRIP IS ANTARCTICA LOGISTICS EXPEDITIONS .... THEY GIVE PREFERENCE TO TEAMS THAT HAVE THREE CHARACTERISTICS.

1) ALE LED TEAMS

2) LARGE THIRD PARTY TEAMS

3) SMALL THIRD PARTY TEAMS

4) "OUR TEAM".

ALE

FINALLY AT 3:30 PM ON DEC. 10TH THE TWIN OTTER AIRCRAFT LIFTED OFF AND HEADED TO BASE CAMP WITH OUR FOUR PERSON TEAM AND FIVE OTHER HIKERS.

almost certainly fatal. The pilots understood that a delayed flight was far better than a fatal crash.

The 100-mile flight to Base Camp took us over mountains and valleys inaccessible to humans. Millions of years of ice, snow, and rock untouched except by the wind stretched below us. Antarctica is so remote its highest peak was not even discovered until 1958—one year before I was born—by a U.S. Navy aircraft. The mountain was named for Carl Vinson, a Congressman from Georgia who served for 50 years and was a key supporter of funding Antarctic research. The first ascent of the massif took place in 1966, 13 years after Sir Edmund Hillary and Tenzing Norgay reached the top of Everest.

The continent was more beautiful than I ever imagined in planning for the expedition. "Vast" didn't come close to describing its scale. Timeless and infinite, it was a landscape of craggy mountains, snow-filled valleys, and endless fields of glaciers and crevasses so deep and blue that they hypnotized me as I gazed down upon them. Most of Antarctica remains a frozen wilderness with little sign of humans. I've run across the Grand Canyon. I've stared out across Africa from the summit of Kilimanjaro. I've biked across the Andes and the Gobi Desert. Nothing compared to the majesty of this frozen continent.

Antarctica was not only remote, it was unique—a lifeless land preserved amid the Cold War in the name of science. The Antarctic Treaty that protects this terrain was signed in 1959. Twelve signatory nations agreed that this uninhabited continent should be a place for only peaceful purposes. Scientific discoveries would be exchanged freely. Territorial claims would be abandoned. Fifty years later, the same nations reaffirmed the treaty and expanded it. They designated the continent as a natural reserve, acknowledging the importance of conserving the species around it and the role Antarctica plays in understanding the world's climate system. They agreed that all human activity, including expeditions like ours, would be conducted in a manner that would promote the continued protection of the Antarctic environment and minimize the impacts upon it.

This day was crystal clear. The plane climbed to 10,000 feet, and as we neared Base Camp, the pilot began circling the landing area. Dozens of black flags flanked the runway. Solar power offered enough electricity to run flight operations, the kitchen, and the dining shelter, but not enough for runway lights. Soon we landed, and the plane heaved and bounced as the skis slammed onto the snow-packed runway, kicking up a fine cloud of white powder. As the haze evaporated, the plane swung around in a semicircle and taxied over to the unloading area. The engines cut, and the snowy fog kicked up by the propellers began to clear. In the distance, the tents of other climbers and the Base Camp's small shelter buildings came into view.

The camp was at an altitude of 7,000 feet, a redoubt the size of a football field at the foot of the Branscombe Glacier, surrounded by snow-capped mountains, crevasse fields, and craggy rock formations. Most teams spend at least 24 hours here to get used to the elevation gain. Feeling like we were running behind, we felt we couldn't afford to wait. We had already been delayed for three days in Punta Arenas, and then we had spent an extra day at Union Glacier. We were feeling strong and ready to push for Low Camp.

We unloaded our gear from the plane onto long, yellow, plastic sleds and dragged them to the outside edges of the landing field. While Chris strode through the snowpack to check in with the camp manager, Mike, Guntis, and I began sorting through our supplies. Some of it we would take with us, while the rest would be left here until our return. Every ounce that we hauled to Low Camp mattered dearly. We would bring our personal items and clothing in our backpacks, each weighing about 30 pounds. The sleds we planned to pull would each weigh an additional 70 pounds. Together they would carry eight duffel bags filled with stoves, food, fuel, cooking gear, and tents. We bound the duffel bags to the sleds using cords, strategically tying knots to attach the sleds to our backpacks. The remaining items we stashed in other duffel bags and buried them in a shallow pit next to the tent camping area, with a bamboo stick to mark the location for when we returned.

Rested and anxious, we attached the sleds to both our packs and the climbing rope before clipping our harnesses into the same line. The rope was essential to protect ourselves and our gear. We would be crossing crevasse fields, where at any time one of us could fall through the snowpack into a deep fissure in the ice. We spaced ourselves 25 feet apart on the 75-foot-long line so that if one of us fell, the weight of the team would save him.

Within an hour of landing, we set out for the mountain. It was 7 p.m., but in the endless daylight of Antarctic summer, we didn't have to worry about nightfall or approaching darkness. By midnight, we figured, we would cover the six miles and 2,100-foot climb to reach Low Camp. As we set out, the tents of Base Camp disappeared behind us. Our heavy mountaineering boots trudged along a well-worn snow path that steadily led us uphill.

Chris set the pace. Once an hour, we stopped for water, food, and a pee break. Poles bearing yellow flags marked where ALE teams had drilled six-inch-wide holes every half-mile, encouraging climbers to urinate with the least environmental impact. Black flags, like the ones that lined the runway, marked the route every 100 yards and clustered together at crevasse crossings. ALE guides created narrow paths to cross the crevasses. A misstep of two feet

B ASE CAMP TO LOW CAMP MAP.
6 MILES. 2100 FT ASCENT

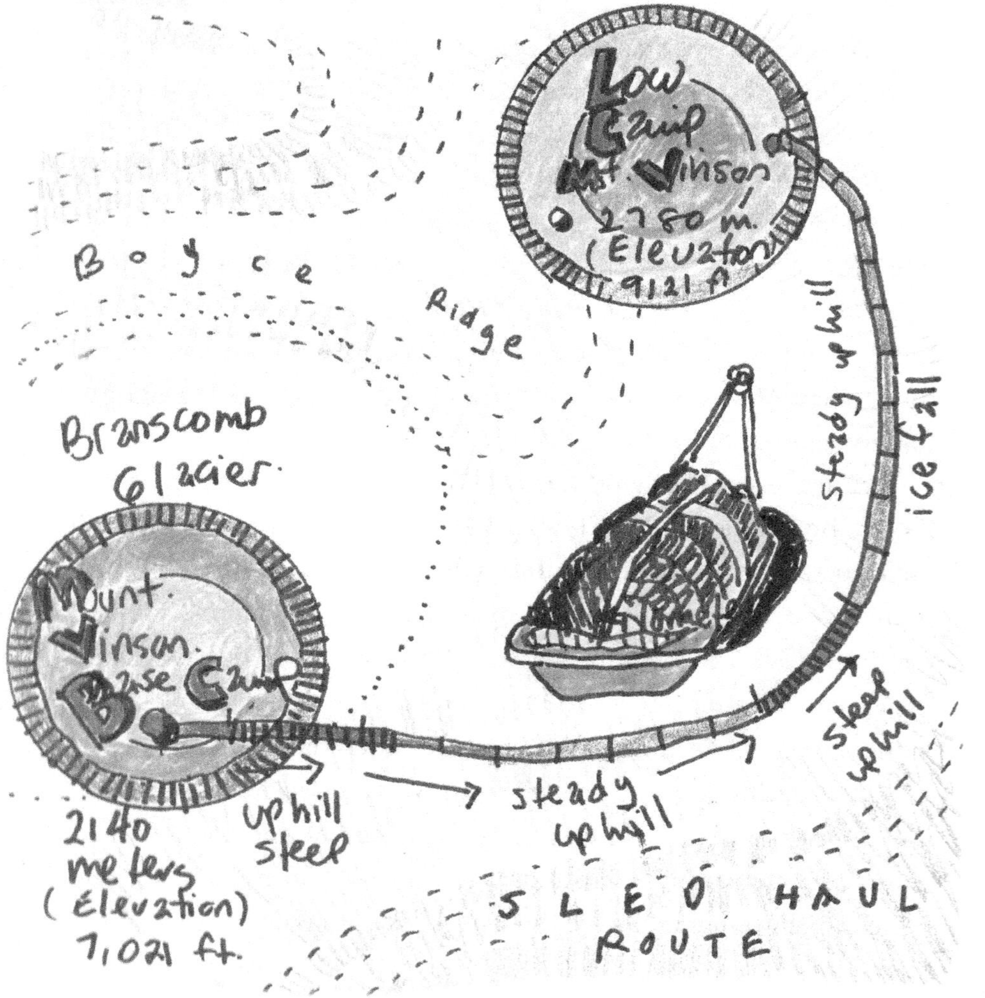

Low Camp
Mt. Vinson
2780 m.
(Elevation)
9121 ft

Boyce

Ridge

Branscomb Glacier

Mount Vinson Base Camp

2140 meters (Elevation) 7,021 ft.

uphill steep

steady uphill

steady uphill

ice fall

steep uphill

S L E D   H A U L
R O U T E

CHRIS   MICHAEL   LEN   CURTIS.

WE PACKED OUR SLEDS AND BACKPACKS
WITH GEAR, CLOTHING, TENTS, KITCHEN GEAR
FOOD, COOKING GAS ETC.   210 KILOS - OR
ROUGHLY 460 LBS - TOTAL.... DISTRIBUTED 70/30
SLED TO BACKPACK.

115 LBS P/PERSON

EACH HIKER DRAGGED AN 80 LB SLED AND
CARRIED A 35 LB BACKPACK!
WE SET OFF AT 7:30 PMM (3 HOURS AFTER
LANDING)

VIEW OF MT
VINSON AND OTHER PEAKS.

WE ARRIVED AT CAMP ONE AT 1:30 AMM HIKING
5.5 MILES OVER 6 HOURS CLIMBING 2300 FT.
I "BONKED" UPON ARRIVAL AT CAMP. ALMOST FELL
                                    OVER!

on either side brought serious danger of falling. After four hours, the pitch steepened. Then the route turned, the terrain leveled, and we reached the base of a broad, windswept valley.

Winds blew against us, causing the temperatures to fall far below zero. To protect ourselves from frostbite, we stopped to change our heavy gloves for down mittens and then resumed the climb. It was a long slog. Roped together, marching slowly, I couldn't help feeling like we resembled a prison chain gang, lurching slowly forward, shouldering heavy packs, pulling the sleds against a bitter wind.

Another hour and we had traversed five miles. In the distance, we could make out points of yellow—the tents of the Amical group from Germany. They had left just a few hours before us. We were almost there, but we had not accounted for the plunging temperatures. The Antarctic sun would not set, but as it circled in the sky it would duck behind the mountains and cast a shadow that would last for six hours. In that shadow, the temperature would plunge 40 degrees.

We arrived at Low Camp at 1 a.m., racing against the clock. We had two hours to set up our tents, fire up our stoves, melt ice, and boil water for dinner before the sunlight faded into shadow. We set up in an unoccupied campsite that offered a flat place to pitch our tents—four-foot-high ice block walls sheltered us from the winds.

My fingers were numb. I was thirsty, hungry, and dizzy, and I fumbled as I tried to fasten the tent poles. Back in Punta Arenas, I could do it in seconds. Without feeling in my fingertips, it was taking precious minutes, and the sun was sliding toward the mountains. The world seemed to be spiraling around me. Whatever dexterity I had just an hour before was gone now. As I tried to drive a bamboo anchor into the ice to secure the tent, I lost my footing and fell backwards, landing squarely in the center of the adjacent tent.

"Forkas, you almost trashed our tent!" Chris shouted.

He was right. I could have easily snapped one of the tent poles in two. With a broken pole, the tent would never withstand a polar windstorm. A simple fumble like this put the entire expedition at risk.

I was hypothermic, but the rapid ascent to 9,000 feet also had made me hypoxic and delusional. Hypoxia comes easily from climbing too high and too fast. In two hours, we had ascended 2,000 feet. My oxygen-starved blood sent my heart rate racing, fogged my brain, and left me gasping for air. My head was spinning. I needed to lay down and rest. Chris ordered me inside the tent and into my sleeping bag. I felt like a failure, incapable of doing the simplest task when the team needed me. My teeth were chattering as I tried to unpack my backpack and retrieve the sleeping bag, the sleeping pad, and the inflatable mattress that would keep me alive on the mountain.

Still in my wet clothes, I fell asleep inside the down bag. When I awoke an hour later, the sun had ducked behind Boyce Ridge, sending temperatures plunging to minus-20. Chris managed to set up a cooking space in the vestibule of our tent. As I peered out from my sleeping bag, where I huddled to stave off hypothermia, I watched as he assembled the stoves and heated water for dinner.

Sensing our desperation, the Amical team walked over from their camp nearby with a Thermos. "We have some hot food if you would like some. It's potato soup," said a middle-aged German woman.

We graciously accepted her offer and appreciated that small act more than we could say. We were exhausted, dehydrated, and suffering from the rapid ascent. It was too cold to cook anything substantial. In the frigid air, the outer fly layer of our tent began to frost over.

We zipped in after eating the soup and fell dead asleep from exhaustion. We didn't emerge until 10 a.m., when the sun reappeared over Boyce Ridge. As the temperature recovered, we set up a cook tent a few yards away over an excavated seating area. Using a handsaw, we cut ice blocks to melt into water for a late breakfast of oatmeal, bacon, powdered eggs, and coffee. The blocks of ice also gave us protection against the wind.

We had made it to Low Camp, but just barely, it seemed. The day would be a rest day for us—a chance to get our bodies used to the altitude. As we lingered in camp, other teams arrived to join us. By day's end, multicolored tents filled the area. Climbers sawed blocks of ice to raise protective walls like ours, turning the camp into a polar construction site. Despite our struggles, team morale began to soar again. We decided that tomorrow, if the weather held, we would set off for High Camp. It was time now to record a video dedication to the Hopecam child we were honoring on our first day of climbing. I brought with me laminated photographs of each child to hold up to the camera while filming. When we returned to civilization, we would post these videos on Hopecam's social media pages and share them with the families of these brave children.

Rahul, age 11 – San Jose, CA

Rahul made a video and emailed it to me before I left for the trip. He is treated at St Jude's. His mom says Rahul knows all the capitals in the world, and since he is very interested in geography, he was very excited that we were traveling to Antarctica. In his picture he is wearing a costume from the movie *The Incredibles*. As we climb the headwall on route to Camp Two, we will be thinking about Rahul, his positive mindset and his no-quit attitude.

DAY THREE

DECEMBER 11TH· TUESDAY

VINSON LOW CAMP · ③

ELEV. 9100 FT.

AT 3:30 LAST NIGHT THE SUN HID BEHIND THE MOUNTAIN RANGE NEAR BASE CAMP FOR 8 HOURS. AND THE TEMPERATURE PLUMMETTED FROM 20 DEGREES TO -20 IN 3 HOURS.

FORTUNATELY WE WERE ABLE TO SET UP A COOKING SPACE IN THE PORTICO OF OUR TENT TO BOIL WATER.

§ § § §

cook stove

foil wind screen

pot

plat form

OUR NEIGHBORING HIKERS CAME OVER AND OFFERED US SOME POTATO SOUP... WHICH SAVED US BECAUSE IT WAS JUST TOO "COLD" TO COOK. WE SET UP AT 2:00 AM

SNOW BLOCK WALL

BAGS

seat-bench

low work-space

COOKING

snow block wall

IN AN ABANDON CAMP SITE USED BY A PREVIOUS TEAM

Mt Vinson Camp One, 12-11-2018

Lots of progress. Flew to Vinson BC and left an hour later. Pulling 70-pound sleds and carrying 30+pound packs to Low Camp 5.6 miles. 2,100 vertical ft. Crazy part was we started the march at 7:30 PM and arrived at 1:30 AM in 24 hours of light!!! But the sun did go behind a peak at 3:30 AM while we were still cooking and melting snow for ice. Insto-brrrrr!!! We snuggled into the sleeping bags until the sun finally returned to heat our tents. As you may have guessed, we are motivated. Hopefully today we can carry some gear up the fixed ropes to High Camp. Rumor has it that a mellow storm may arrive in the next 24 hours. Team is doing great. (Chris Warner)

Mt Vinson Camp One, 12-11-2018

Weather update: Stable thru at least Friday. -26c is the high temp. 5-10 knot winds. Plan is to move to High Camp on the 12th (12,402 feet), 8-hour climb. 13th is Vinson summit day, 9-12 hour round trip. Team is pumped, and they will need to be as this is 2 hard days in a row! Great to be with a strong and motivated team. Time for bed. (Chris Warner)

Lesson 3: Overconfidence often has consequences.

By moving to Camp One late in the evening, we threaded a very narrow needle. The temperatures plummeted just after we had our camp established. A slight delay in arrivals would have put all of us at risk of severe frostbite and hypothermia. Chris had led 200 international expeditions over a 30-year career, but this was his first time climbing in Antarctica. He was overly influenced by teammates who were anxious to get moving, despite his better judgment.

DAY ④

DECEMBER
12th 2018
CAMP ONE
RECOVERY DAY.

AFTER A VERY LONG DAY TUESDAY
ARRIVING TO BASE CAMP VIA THE TWIN
ENGINE OTTER, PACKING SLEDS AND
ARRIVING VERY LATE, WE DECIDED TO
USE WEDNESDAY AS A RECOVERY
DAY. AT 9,100 FEET ABOVE SEA LEVEL
WE NEEDED A DAY TO ACCLIMATE.

AT 1:00 PM WE SET OFF BUT HAD TO
TURN BACK 15 MIN LATER DUE TO HIGH
WINDS EXCEEDING 30 MPH.
ON THE HEAD
WALL.

CHRIS AND
I SET OFF TO HIKE
AS FAR UP THE
HEAD WALL TO
MAKE A GEAR
DROP... FUEL, EXTRA
FOOD, CLOTHING THAT
WE WOULD NEED IN HIGH
CAMP.

CHAPTER FOUR
DECEMBER 12

"Trust instinct to the end, even though you can give no reason."
Ralph Waldo Emerson

THE NEXT MORNING, OUR TEAM BEGAN breaking down our tents and dividing the 200 pounds of food, fuel, supplies, and gear we would need for the summit bid into four equal amounts, one allotment for each of us. Climbing is an equitable sport, and we would carry equal shares. By noon our packs were full. We clamped the crampons to our boots, clicked and locked carabiners connecting our harnesses to the team rope, and set off to the headwall that would take us to High Camp in one single push.

We ascended along the northern end of Branscomb Ridge, looking across at Mount Shinn and the glaciers below, to the base of the headwall. The 2,000-foot slope rose above us, becoming steeper and steeper as it climbed. As we prepared to clip to the fixed rope system that ran up the slope, Chris gazed skyward. He frowned. High above, lenticular clouds were beginning to form and swirl about.

"We're turning around," he said. "I don't like the look of those clouds. Too much wind at the top."

The clouds looked harmless to me—fragile wisps of white in a blue sky. But I trusted Chris, and I knew Mike and Guntis felt the same. Over his 30-year career, he had led more than 200 expeditions on some of the world's most challenging peaks. If he said turn around, who was I to second-guess him?

Heading back didn't mean our day was done. This was where my job as mule came in. At Low Camp, we broke down our packs again, but this time we separated out two backpacks and loaded them with just enough gear, food, and fuel for three days—the supplies we would need for a summit bid and nothing else. Chris had a plan. He and I would push up the headwall and cache the gear two-thirds of the way up. It would be a haul for the two of us, but it would lighten the team's load when conditions were right to climb to High Camp. When the weather cleared and the four of us reached the top of the ropes, we would collect the gear for the final push to High Camp.

While Guntis and Mike stayed behind to re-establish our camp, Chris and I roped up and returned to the headwall. We clipped our jumars into the fixed ropes that snaked up the slope and started our ascent. If Chris was right about the winds, we wouldn't have much time to stash our gear before the weather turned foul.

Indeed, the winds became stronger and stronger as we ascended. After an hour, we approached the halfway point—a large outcrop nicknamed the picnic rocks. It seemed like a grim spot for a picnic. Winds were gusting down the mountain, making it impossible to move on.

"I can't feel my face," I shouted to Chris, my voice barely audible in the howling wind.

This was as far as we would get today, we decided. With numb fingers, we unloaded our gear into big waterproof bags, tied them together and secured them between several black boulders along the trail. With gale-force winds beginning to funnel down the

- TENTS   2 × 8 lbs   16 lbs
- STOVES   2 × 4 lbs   8 lbs
- FUEL TANKS 4 + 2 GAL.   16 lbs
- FOOD   6 DAYS.   100 lbs
- PICKETS. & TENT POLES   8 lbs
- ROPES   30 lbs
- SHOVEL, SAW, TOOLS, KITCHEN   17 lbs
  POTS AND PANS   _____
                                        200 LBS

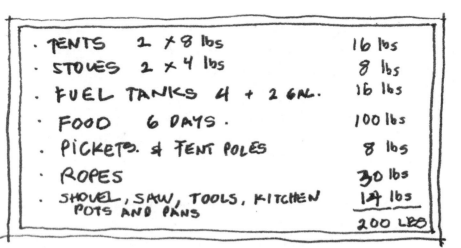

STARTING AT 2:30 PM WE SET OFF CARRYING 40 POUNDS EACH OF GEAR.
WITH HIGH WINDS 30 MPH GOT TO 1/2 WAY
ROCK EDGE
DROPPED GEAR HERE
9300 ft. BOTTOM OF FIXED ROPES.
ELEVATION 11,400 TOP OF FIXED ROPES.
Headwall

AT 5:00 PM WE RETURNED TO BASE CAMP
GUNTIS & MICHAEL HAD RE ESTABLISHED OUR
CAMP AND HAD DINNER UNDERWAY.

① 3.18 mile climb. up ropes
② 6 hours total time.
③ 2,470 feet ascent
④ Avg HR : 135 Bpm. beats p/minute

comparison ?
36 mile run...or
100 mile bike ride

mountainside, we descended the ropes and retreated to Low Camp. When we arrived, I was relieved to see Guntis and Mike had set up our tents and had dinner cooking in the mess tent.

Mt Vinson Camp One, 12-12-2018

We packed up and headed to High Camp, but the winds turned ugly, so back to camp. Guntis and Michael spent the afternoon rebuilding the camp. Len and I ferried loads up the fixed ropes to a rocky outcrop halfway to High Camp. The high winds grew stronger and combined with the -15c temps the cold was brutal. Michael & Guntis made us dinner while we crawled into the tents to warm up. If the weather improves, we will try to move to High Camp. Currently blowing at 25 knots and gusting to 35 knots. Classic Antarctica. Time to burrow into the sleeping bags. (Chris Warner)

Genesis, age 12 – Albuquerque, NM

On the second day we climbed for Genesis, a young girl fighting leukemia. She learned she had leukemia after a visit to her primary care doctor—just like my family's experience. She is an active student and athlete and the Hopecam connection made a big difference in her life with frequent zoom calls with her classmates and teammates at school.

The following morning, we saw more lenticular clouds building at the top of Mount Vinson, a sure sign of more high winds, and it was an easy decision to stay put and wait for better weather. We decided to make another attempt at getting our gear to the top of the ropes. This time, Guntis joined Chris and me, and we set off to

DAY FIVE (5)

High Wind

NO CLIMB DAY
CAMP ONE

...another frustrating day waiting for the weather to clear on the mountain.

..swirling circular lenticular clouds

ice block walls

LENTICULAR CLOUDS SWIRLING IN CIRCULAR FORMATIONS HIGH IN THE ATMOSPHERE ARE NOT GOOD NEWS FOR OUR TEAM. TODAY

SINCE CAMP ONE IS AT 2780 METERS WE ARE BEGINNING THE PROCESS OF ACCLIMATIZING TO HIGHER ELEVATIONS AS WE ASCEND.

SECOND GEAR HAUL

CHRIS, GUNTIS AND MYSELF SET OFF ON THE ROPES TO MOVE OUR DROPPED GEAR FROM THE "LUNCH STOP" 1/2 WAY UP THE ROPES.

WE DIVIDED THE 60 ± POUNDS OF FOOD, FUEL, SUPPLIES AND GEAR AND HAULED IT TO THE TOP OF THE ROPES. HOWLING WINDS PUSHED DOWN THE MOUNTAIN MAKING IT ONE OF THE MOST COLD AND BITTER CLIMBS I HAVE EXPERIENCED. SIX HOURS AFTER DEPARTING CAMP, WE RETURNED TO LOW CAMP PASSING THE AMICAL TEAM WHO WERE SETTING OFF TO HIGH CAMP.

the headwall to gather our gear from the picnic rocks, cache it at the top of the ropes, and get back to camp in time for dinner.

As we arrived at the bottom of the ropes to start our ascent, we paused for a water break. I kept my one-liter Nalgene water bottle stashed in an insulated cover clipped to my backpack. As I pulled it out, the bottle slipped from my glove and dropped to the ice. Like a rocket, it slid down the slope, accelerating rapidly. The bottle reached terminal velocity within seconds and vanished from sight. That bottle was very important. I'd only brought three with me. Now only two remained.

"On the mountain you will never get more than you have," Guntis said. "Only less."

The simple wisdom struck me. Anything we needed we would carry ourselves. Anything we lost would be gone for good. Fortunately, I thought, I dropped the bottle at the bottom of the ropes. If it had fallen from higher ground, such a simple error could have had deadly consequences. Bounding downhill at speeds better than 50 miles an hour, the bottle could have severely injured a climber below. Thankfully, we were just moving gear today and we would be back at Low Camp soon enough. If we were heading to High Camp, I could have faced serious dehydration. The fumble was the sort of thing I call a "stupid tax"—the price you pay for inexperience when you find yourself in a new environment in life or business. Fortunately, this time, it was a small price to pay.

An hour later, we arrived at the picnic rocks, and we found our supplies securely stashed amid the boulders just as we had left them. Stuffing the contents into our backpacks, we headed back to the ropes. The winds howled on the upper mountain as we progressed slowly up the headwall. My goggles fogged in the cold as I followed Chris and Guntis up the knife-edge ridge leading to the top of the ropes. I took off the goggles and from my front pocket removed the fabric to clean them. In the seconds it took to find the fabric, the moisture inside the lens froze into a thin layer of ice. After scraping out the ice and putting on the goggles, the lens froze again. My vision was reduced to the size of a pinhole. Soon, even that was gone. The moisture from the thin fabric buff, which I had wrapped around my neck and chin to protect my nose from frost-bite, was causing the goggles to fog. My only hope of seeing was to remove it. Given the choice between wind burn and blindness, I chose wind burn. I was on a steep slope with 40 pounds of gear in my pack in a total whiteout, inching up a steep ice wall. I had to concentrate. I had to see what was a step or two in front of me.

Reaching the top of the ropes, we unclipped and found a sheltered outcropping to store our provisions until we could return on our final ascent to High Camp. We transferred the gear into heavy plastic bags, secured them again between rocks and began our descent. Reaching the bottom of the ropes we stopped, unclipped, and trudged the last half-mile to camp. Four climbers from the Amical team passed us on the narrow path, fully loaded, heading to High Camp. Chris stopped to warn the lead guide. Our experience at the top wasn't one we would wish on anyone.

"The winds are blowing horizontally at the top of the ropes," he said. "We never made it to Camp Two with our gear and had to turn back at the top of the ropes."

The Amical guide waved Chris off.

"It's really bad up there—way worse than I expected," Chris continued. "You sure you want to go up now?"

The guide assured him he knew what he was doing. The team continued on. "That's one overconfident guide," Chris said.

Chris had learned a valuable lesson on our first day's climb:

Listen to the other guides. The Amical guide would later discover the consequences of overconfidence.

After four hours of wind and cold on the headwall, we found Mike at Low Camp ready with Thermoses of coffee and a hot meal in the cook tent. The expression on Mike's face was worrisome as he watched us trudge single file back to our campsite. Did we really appear that beat up? To Mike, we did. To him, we could have been that doomed party of explorers who were at the South Pole with adventurer Robert Falcon Scott in 1912, ones who were so beaten down by the effort that they soon died.

Unlike those poor souls, though, we would be fine. We just needed some rest. Exhausted, we crawled into our sleeping bags.

Mt Vinson Camp One, 12-13-2018
Woke up to high winds on the ridge above us. Impossible to move High Camp. But at 3 PM the wind slowed and Guntis, Len and I climbed the fixed ropes moving all the food and fuel and some personal gear to 11,000 feet. Unfortunately, the winds surged halfway up the ropes to 20 to 25 knots blowing ice crystals into any bit of exposed skin. Temps were -10 to -20 Fahrenheit we are definitely getting a true Antarctic experience. Michael stayed behind to make us dinner and hot drinks. It takes a team to climb Vinson. Especially in these conditions. Everyone is making sacrifices for the team. Spirits are high. Too bad the temps are not! We are now cocooning in warm sleeping bags. Tomorrow will be another adventure. (Chris Warner)

Our third day at Low Camp was about rest, recovery, and adjustment. Our bodies were slowly acclimatizing to the thinner air of high elevation. "Climb high, sleep low" is the mountaineering mantra for preparing your body for the stress of high altitude. Stashing our gear at 11,000 feet and returning to camp at 9,000 feet had been a struggle, but our bodies were benefiting from it. All except for my nose. Leaving it uncovered to keep my goggles from steaming up, I suffered from a very severe wind burn. Studying it in a pocket mirror and selfies on my iPhone, I counted six different shades of red, brown, and black blistered skin. I had some moisturizer and antibacterial ointment in my first-aid kit, so I addressed my condition as best I could. I was lucky it wasn't frostbitten.

Our wait brought good news from the camp director down at Union Glacier. Weather forecasters said the winds at the top of Mount Vinson were decreasing. Tomorrow promised good conditions to climb. The word spread fast through the other teams at Low Camp. By noon the next day, every climber there had packed up, preparing to move by midday. We broke down our camp, filled our backpacks, and put on our climbing boots and crampons, ready to move.

By the time we reached the headwall, I was feeling confident. This was my third time on the ropes and ascending with a heavy pack using the jumar had become comfortable. The sun was shining. The air was still. It seemed like a perfect day for climbing. We made the long ascent in good shape. At the top of the ropes, our stashed gear was waiting for us in the rocks.

The conditions didn't hold out for long, however. Too soon the wind kicked up, blowing a fine mist of snow into the sky, causing a whiteout. Our visibility fell to less than 50 feet and temperatures plunged as well. It was time to divide our supplies even further, Chris said. We would take just half of these supplies to High Camp, less than a mile away. The other half would wait for us here. That would allow us to make better time to camp.

DAY SIX
LOW
HIGH
FRIDAY 12.M

DAY
6

WEATHER
IMPROVED TODAY
WITH LIGHT WINDS
THAT ALLOWED OUR
TEAM TO MOVE
FROM LOW
CAMP TO HIGH CAMP.

TOP OF
ROPES
VIEW

LEN
BOOTS

WE TRAVELLED + 3 MILES & 2,000 + FEET UP THE
MOUNTAIN TO A WINDY PLATEAU

CHRIS SILOUETTE
AT TOP &
ROPES.

WE WERE
UNABLE TO TRANSPORT ALL &
OUR "STASH" TO THE HIGH CAMP, PLANNING
FOR A RETURN ROUND TRIP THE NEXT DAY

LOW CAMP TO HIGH CAMP
2 MILES · 3,281 FT. ASCENT

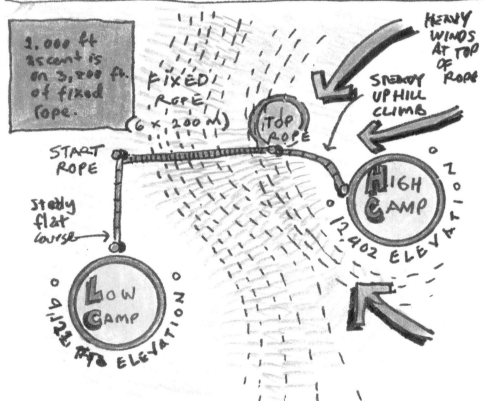

1,000 ft ascent is on 3,800 ft. of fixed rope.

FIXED ROPE (6 × 200 M)

HEAVY WINDS AT TOP OF ROPE

STEADY UPHILL CLIMB

TOP ROPE

START ROPE

Steady flat course →

HIGH CAMP

12,402 ELEVATION

LOW CAMP

9,121 FT. ELEVATION

LOW CAMP TO HIGH CAMP IS THE MOST TECHNICALLY DEMANDING SECTION ON THE CLIMB WITH ALMOST A MILE ON FIXED ROPES ENDING WITH FIERCE DOWNHILL WINDS.

As we continued upward, the slope steepened and the winds grew even stronger, blowing razors of snow straight at us. Our extremities were the first to feel the impact. Stopping briefly to swap from gloves to heavier mittens, I noticed a black object sliding quickly toward me. It was Mike's mitten—barreling at me like a bowling ball. He must have forgotten to tether the strap to his wrist, and it had somehow slipped from his grasp.

I instinctively dropped to my knees and tackled it. I felt like I was recovering a fumble in a high school football game. I thought of how quickly my water bottle rocketed down the mountain the day before. A seemingly small mistake can have brutal consequences on the mountain. Like Guntis said, you will never get more than you have up here. Had I missed the mitten, it could have slid off the ridge and disappeared into the void. Mike's chance to summit might have vanished with it. Cinching the rope, I walked toward him and returned the mitten.

"Len had leaped on it with all fours," a thankful Mike later recalled, "like a mother bear protecting its cub from a wolf pack."

By mid-afternoon, after a seven-hour climb, we finally arrived at a blustery and windswept High Camp. Despite the severe conditions, it was a magnificent sight and one I will never forget. The camp sits on a plateau about 800 feet below the col of Mount Shinn, the fourth highest peak in Antarctica, just 200 feet shorter than Vinson. In the distance lies the Branscomb Glacier and the Jacobsen Valley. We had no time to take in more of the view, though. At over 12,000 feet, the wind was bitter cold, and once we stopped climbing, our core temperatures began to fall.

We began to assemble our tents, but the wind and cold made it nearly impossible. Snapping the delicate plastic clips around the carbon fiber poles and threading the poles through the fragile nylon tent layers required a finesse that our frozen hands and oversized mittens didn't allow. If we lost our grip, the tent would become airborne, blowing into oblivion like a lost kite.

I saw Guntis was struggling, much as I had on our first night at Low Camp. Eight years earlier, he experienced a debilitating injury on an expedition to Makalu, in the Himalayas. Descending from the summit for camp, Guntis stopped to retrieve a fresh cylinder of oxygen when he encountered a doctor assisting a climber in distress. At the doctor's request, Guntis unselfishly surrendered his last oxygen cylinder to the climber. But without oxygen at 8,000 meters, Guntis became disoriented and needed to dig out a snow cave to rest before making his way back to camp. The experience left him with excruciating frostbite on multiple fingers and the eventual loss of the top portion of his thumb. The trauma of frostbite doesn't end when the heat returns, though. Frostbite has a memory. Once you are afflicted with it, your body has a difficult time functioning in the same way again. The memory of that moment refuses to leave you alone. After trying in vain, Guntis had to leave the tent assembly to Chris, Mike, and me while he unpacked our cooking gear from the backpacks.

By working together, we got the tents up in a half-hour. With our gear secure inside them, it was time for dinner. I agreed to get the stove running in the small vestibule of the tent to heat up our freeze-dried food pouches. I attached the foot-long fuel cylinder to the burner, opened the valve, bled a small amount of liquid gas to prime the burner, and struck a match. Flames erupted into the vestibule, nearly scorching the top of the tent. I had released too much fuel. I immediately cut the supply, but the flame didn't die out. Chris instinctively grabbed a frying pan and held it over the flame, keeping it from reaching the ceiling tent fabric. If it had, the nylon tent would have burned in seconds.

FRIDAY   12 · 14 · 18

AFTER ASCENDING 3,281 FT
WE ARRIVED AT HIGH CAMP
PERCHED ON A LARGE ESCARPMENT.

HIGH CAMP WINDS WERE
Brutal!

20-30 knot winds + -10 degrees
meant temperatures were below
-30 f.... this place was colder than
anyplace I've been. Arriving at
high camp after a long uphill battle
with the fixed ropes and assembling
tents with cold, high wind was
a tough ending to a very long day.

It was another small mistake that could have proved disastrous for our entire team. Had the tent caught fire, the four of us would have to spend the rest of the expedition huddled together in a single three-person tent. I promised to volunteer for less technical tasks. *What did my teammates think*, I wondered? *Had I become a liability to the expedition?* In one day, I had tackled Mike's mitten and saved him from frostbite, but I nearly burned down our tent.

We awoke after a fitful sleep to brutal winds that hammered our tents into the morning. Stepping outside, we put the temperature at around minus-30, but it was just a guess. After leading so many expeditions, Chris purposefully did not bring a thermometer.

"I would rather *not* know how cold it is," he said over breakfast of coffee and oatmeal. "It will just make us depressed looking at the number."

Antarctica, he said, was by far the coldest place he had ever been.

But despite another day of wind and cold, and even though we would not be summiting today, Chris told us we still had plenty to do. He wanted to haul up the supplies we had stashed in the rocks. "C'mon," he said. "It's time to put on our big-boy pants and retrieve our food supplies."

Mt Vinson Camp Two, 12-14-2018
Made it to High Camp! A seven-hour climb with big packs. It was pretty calm until the last hour when the wind hit a sustained 15+ knots and bitter cold -25 Fahrenheit. Setting up the tents was a lesson in teamwork, everyone slept soundly. But first, Len and I must drop down the hill for about 600 feet to collect the food we stashed yesterday. Thank goodness he is an endurance athlete. I'm putting him to work! (Chris Warner)

SATURDAY **DEC 15,** 2018
HIGH CAMP · MT. VINSON MASSIF

RECOVERY DAY

WITH FIERCE 20+ KNOT
WINDS BLOWING AT HIGH
CAMP, NO ONE COULD MOVE

DAY
7

WITHOUT TAKING TREMENOUS
RISK ON GETTING FROSTBITE

HOWEVER
OUR FEAR-
LESS
LEADER
CHRIS
WARNER
SAYS " ITS TIME TO PUT ON OUR BIG BOY
PANTS AND HEAD BACK TO THE TOP OF
THE ROPES AND FINISH OUR HAUL BACK
TO HIGH CAMP WITH OUR FOOD SUPPLIES.

WE FINISHED AFTER 2:35 AND 1.43 MILES
OF CLIMBING WITH FOOD FOR 3 DAYS.

We would bring just a single backpack for the 50-pound load. Chris offered to carry it.

"We will go faster with me carrying the pack," he said.

We descended back to the top of the headwall to our supply stash, loaded the pack, and turned back for High Camp. Chris carried the load, but although he was working hard to disguise it, I could tell he was struggling under the weight. At the halfway mark, I urged him to let me take a turn. I was the designated mule, after all. Besides, carrying the pack made me feel better about almost burning down our tent. Chris agreed. He unbuckled the pack. I swung it onto my back, cinched the waist strap, and trudged on. In an hour we were back at camp with enough food to last us for three additional days, if we needed it. And we just might. It was hard to say when we would be able to try for the summit. The fierce winds made it almost impossible to move. Snow accumulated around our tents, burying the top of our tent stakes. A heavy crust of ice formed over the snowpack, covering the skirts of our tents. I dreaded the thought of chipping it away to excavate our tents when it was time to descend.

The camp looked to me like an icy version of Mars—lifeless, desolate, but beautiful. It was a forbidding place, in every elemental way. Winds can reach 200 miles an hour here at the worst times of year. Temperatures regularly plunge far below zero. Frostbite will burn your skin, but so can the endless summer sun. In the 52 years since the first expedition to Mount Vinson, almost my entire lifetime, fewer than 3,000 people have ever reached this camp. I was thrilled to be one of them.

Mt Vinson Camp Two, 12-15-2018

Nonstop wind through the night and into the afternoon. Will it stop? Len and I did the final carry of gear we had stashed a few hundred feet below High Camp 2+ hour trip in brutal temps and a 20-knot winds. When we came back Michael had boiling water ready, then hot food. Everyone is trapped at High Camp hoping for a summit attempt tomorrow. The theme for this trip is fierce weather making even the easy tasks hard. Time to hibernate in our tents. (Chris Warner)

The Amical team was gone when we arrived. Still headstrong after their push to reach High Camp, they attempted to summit amid the windstorm. As the day wore on, our concern for them grew. They were still on the mountain when we fell asleep. I thought of the hot food they had offered us our first, fragile night on the mountain. I had nothing to offer them now, wherever they were, except prayers for a safe return.

Lesson 4: Trust your gut.

In Malcolm Gladwell's acclaimed book *Blink: The Power of Thinking Without Thinking*, the author writes of experts making accurate decisions in split seconds without ever stopping to think why. It's how a firefighter knows when to leave a burning building before an imminent collapse. Chris' gut feeling after seeing the lenticular clouds forming above saved us from near disaster.

CHAPTER FIVE
DECEMBER 16

"The purpose of life is not to be happy. It is to be useful, to be honorable, to be compassionate, to have it make some difference that you have lived and lived well."

Ralph Waldo Emerson

WHEN I AWOKE, BONE-CHILLING WINDS continued to buffet High Camp. I didn't want to leave the shelter of my warm tent. I couldn't imagine making a push for the summit. It would be a frontal assault against frostbite and hypothermia.

The guides in camp were worried. The Amical team had yet to return after 20 hours on the mountain. But just as the ALE guides prepared to mount a rescue, the Amical team stumbled back into camp. The push to the summit from High Camp and the return usually takes nine or 10 hours. The Amical team had labored for 16 hours on the mountain before turning back 1,500 feet shy of the peak. Hurricane-force winds and temperatures below minus-40 had proven to be too much, ending their summit attempt. They staggered into High Camp exhausted, dehydrated, and hypothermic. Some sought treatment for severe frostbite. One climber's nose was turning black.

We didn't want to suffer a similar fate, but our window to summit was closing fast. Chris consulted with the ALE guides. Their weather forecasters at Union Glacier are the best in the world, and they had more experience than anyone dealing with the fierce conditions of Antarctica. Despite the severe conditions at camp, the guides were remarkably optimistic. An ALE scouting team of two guides left camp earlier that morning and reported that, while high winds were blasting our camp, the conditions at the summit may be far different. At 9 a.m., one guide radioed his observations. About a mile from camp, the winds surprisingly had abated. From that point forward, it looked like calm air and clear skies.

Word spread quickly through camp. Our summit attempt was a go. We prepared our packs with just enough water, fuel, and gear to reach the summit and return. Our gear included our heaviest fleeces, down parkas, windproof jackets, down gloves, and goggles in case the weather suddenly turned again. With ice axes in hand, we secured our crampons and shouldered our packs. Our packs were as light as they had ever been on this expedition. We wanted to be fast and nimble on our way to the summit. Three teams departed ahead of us. Two more would follow. When we set out at 10 a.m., the Amical team members were in their tents, exhausted after their ill-fated attempt.

Our first half-mile up the mountain was pure agony. Battering winds blew straight at us, and we struggled to move at all. We had difficulty simply catching our breath and our faces burned with cold. Then, as the route turned east toward a saddle between the mountains flanking Vinson, the winds faded away to nothing. We appeared to be out of the worst of it.

In the lead, Chris set a steady pace. The route to the summit

Mount Vinson
SUMMIT DAY
4.3 mi @ 16,050

- Sunday
- December 16th.
- Day ⑧ High camp 12,402 ft.

WITH A WINDY START A HIGH CAMP AFTER A LONG AND PROTRACTED WIND STORM WE SET OFF FOR THE SUMMIT WITHIN 30 MINUTES THE SUN WARMED UP TO 50+ DEGREES AS WE HIKED ACROSS GOODGE COL TOWARD THE VINSON MASSIF.

(Curtis)

(Len)

(mike)

WE WILL ASCEND 3,648 FEET FROM HIGH CAMP TO THE TOP OF VINSON

[NEARING RIDGE LINE]

THE LAST 100 FEET ARE ALONG A STEEP RIDGE OVERLOOKING BASE CAMP.

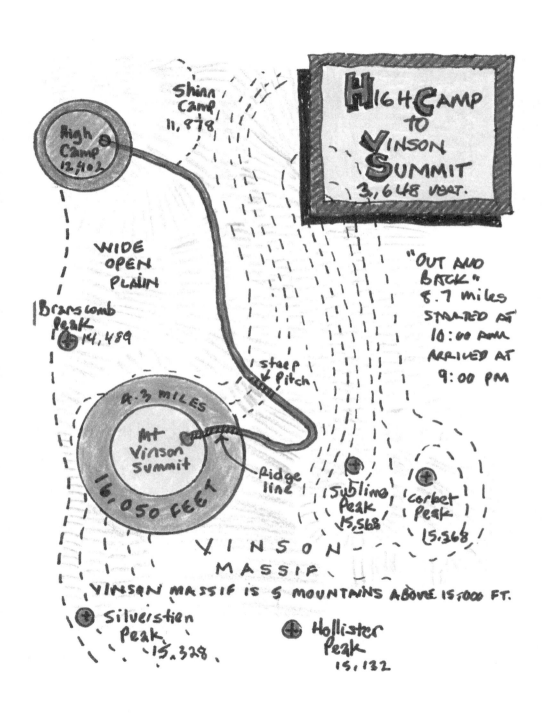

Shinn Camp
11,878

High Camp
12,402

HIGH CAMP
TO
VINSON
SUMMIT
3,648 vert.

WIDE
OPEN
PLAIN

Branscomb
Peak
14,489

"OUT AND
BACK"
8.7 miles
STARTED AT
10:00 AM
ARRIVED AT
9:00 PM

steep
↓ pitch

4.3 MILES

Mt
Vinson
Summit

16,050 FEET

Ridge
line

Sublime
Peak
15,568

Corbet
Peak
15,368

VINSON
MASSIF

VINSON MASSIF IS 5 MOUNTAINS ABOVE 15,000 FT.

Silverstien
Peak
15,328

Hollister
Peak
15,132

shot up 4,000 vertical feet and down again on a nine-mile round trip. We sweated in the sun, peeling off layers until the winds picked up and we put them back on again. Every hour, Chris halted us for a five-minute break—a chance to change layers, eat a snack, drink from our water bottles, and rest before moving on. Dehydration was a serious challenge now. Unscrewing a water bottle with heavy mittens was so difficult, it was practically impossible to stop for a sip on our own without tugging on our team members roped with us. We would all have to stop and drink together.

This routine, forced to work so much in tandem, was difficult for me. As an endurance athlete, I felt prepared for the physical challenge of climbing Mount Vinson, but my background was in solo sports. I was used to taking a water break whenever I wanted. Even when I had a team supporting me, my breaks were my decision. Here, I was roped to my teammates. Everything we did we had to do together. We were all struggling to find an even pace, and Chris was growing frustrated.

Even bathroom breaks were a communal affair. For me, that was becoming urgent. I should have used the latrine back at High Camp, but leaving my warm tent to squat over a drywall bucket behind a snow block wall, exposed to the wind, was more than I could muster. During our final break before reaching the summit I explained my dilemma to my teammates. Chris handed me a thick, gray plastic bag designed for human waste. Guntis's motto—that the mountain only takes away—was true for climbers, too. Everything we brought to Antarctica had to return to Chile. Everything. Every human activity on the continent required a special permit from the National Science Foundation. Every possible impact was measured, from the carbon dioxide emitted by our flights to the removal of our waste.

I took off my mittens and my pack, unclipped from the rope, and descended to a relatively secluded area. Out of view of the others, I unclipped my harness and three layers of pants, took aim at a plastic bag, and upon finishing, reversed the process. This was taking valuable time. My teammates waited patiently, but they were getting colder as each second passed. I hurried back and pulled on my mittens. As I tugged the wrist straps with my teeth, I heard a click. A small piece of my front tooth broke off and disappeared into the snow. My tooth's frigid enamel was another victim of Vinson's weather and Guntis's motto. Mine wasn't the only delay. As a team we hadn't found our cadence—the fastest, most efficient way up the mountain. As a result, things were becoming more dire. Too often we were idle, or nearly so, in the frigid temperatures and our core temperatures were tumbling. All of us began to shiver. We would soon become hypothermic if we didn't get moving quickly.

Chris was worried. His experience as a guide had taught him that expeditions rarely failed from one mistake. Usually, failure was the result of the compounding effects of a series of small errors.

Chris's steady pace brought us to a rocky platform just a few hundred feet below the summit. We were much more exposed here. The winds picked up. The temperatures plunged. We followed the platform to a line of exposed rock and onward to the knife edge ridge that led to the summit. Steel pickets pounded deep into the snow at 10-meter intervals stretched along the ridge. We clipped our team rope in and prepared for the last, most dangerous stretch.

On either side of us, the mountain fell away to the ice sheet thousands of feet below. The summit was in plain view, and our hearts raced as we pushed along the deadly ridge. The sunlight striking the swirling snow formed a halo above the summit, appearing almost spiritual. Months of planning and training, hundreds of logistical actions, and days of hauling hundreds of pounds of supplies up this mountain were now distilled into these final steps.

Just a few hundred yards were all that separated us from the summit. Antarctica's other great peaks—Mount Gardner, Tyree, Epperly—towered around us. Above, the sun circled endlessly in crystalline blue. As we scrambled along the outcrop, our crampons clattered uselessly against the exposed rocks, leading us step by step to the peak.

At 6 p.m., we arrived.

All our efforts had finally brought us here. We were standing on the summit at the bottom of the world. We took off our packs and celebrated with hugs, fist bumps, and broad smiles. The view overlooking the polar peaks around was glorious, and we snapped pictures of ourselves holding ice axes high overhead. Mike brought a flag from the International Medical Corps. Andy Cole, the Adventure Consultant team leader who took me to task back at Union Glacier Camp, had summited just minutes before us. He held up a professional camera and captured an image of our team basking in the glory of the summit.

I had dedicated each day of this journey to a Hopecam child, but this day was special. I unpacked the laminated photo of Derreon, the young girl this day was dedicated to. Using my iPhone, Mike videoed the dedication at 16,020 feet. The four of us posed for pictures, then moved aside. Other climbers were waiting.

SUMMIT DAY WAS SUNNY AND
MOSTLY WARM WITH ALMOST
NO WIND. THE AFTERNOON TEMPS
WERE ABOVE 40° AND THE STEADY
UPHILL EFFORT REQUIRED SWAPPING
LAYERS WHEN THE WINDS SLOWLY
STARTED TO LOWER THE AIR TEMPS

DAY 8

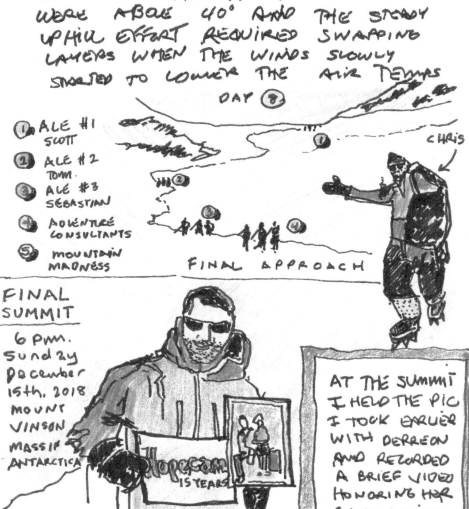

① ALE #1
   SCOTT
② ALE #2
   TOM
③ ALE #3
   SEBASTIAN
④ ADVENTURE
   CONSULTANTS
⑤ MOUNTAIN
   MADNESS

CHRIS

FINAL APPROACH

FINAL
SUMMIT

6 P.M.
Sunday
December
15th, 2018
MOUNT
VINSON
MASSIF
ANTARCTICA

AT THE SUMMIT
I HELD THE PIC
I TOOK EARLIER
WITH DERREON
AND RECORDED
A BRIEF VIDEO
HONORING HER
FIGHT AGAINST
WILMS TUMOR

Derreon, age 6 – Gainesville, VA

Derreon is a six-year-old girl being treated for Wilms tumor, a rare disease that affects the kidneys and pancreas. Derreon and her mom met me at Inova Hospital in Northern Virginia in November. I brought some of the technical gear I would use during the climb and explained how the ice axe, boots, crampons, and other tools all have a purpose during different sections of the climb. She was curious about Antarctica and asked if I expected to see any penguins during my visit. I told Derreon that I planned to bring a photo of her with me to display on the day that our team reached the summit. Leaving the pediatric radiation department with my climbing gear I realized that her battle with cancer was unrelenting. Thirty consecutive days of radiation had left her exhausted, and her treatment would extend well into 2019. Another observation: It's not a very good idea to yield an ice axe while walking through a children's hospital.

With one last look across the peaks of Antarctica, we shouldered our packs for the descent back to camp. In my rush to rejoin the team after my bathroom break, I now realized, I had not properly secured my harness. One slip and I could have plummeted off the ridge or into a crevasse. Fortunately, I noticed my mistake—and my teammates didn't. As is often the case with high-altitude climbs, the descent can prove more dangerous than the hard journey to the top had been. As mountaineers like to say, "Ascending is optional, but descending is mandatory." More climbers perish on the way down than the way up. The rigorous climb drains their energy and saps their concentration, and they pay the price on the return. I didn't want to be one of them.

Our descent proved swift and smooth. The weather was clear. The winds were calm. On the ascent, my eyes were fixed on the route. On the way down the gently sloping trail, our team was ebullient, smiling like little kids. The swift return was joyous, and the endless vistas that surrounded us fed our souls. High peaks stretched into the distance. As expedition teams heading up passed us on the trail, we shared words of encouragement. Every downward step brought more oxygen to our lungs and more energy to our bodies. We stopped often, posing for pictures and laughing. It was the most lighthearted moment of the journey.

Soon, though, the mountain reminded us who was in charge. Less than a mile from High Camp, the winds we had fought on the ascent returned, and they increased in velocity and power as we approached our tents. The sun ducked behind the base of the mountain, and the temperatures plunged in the resulting shade. The sting of the wind on our faces quickly reminded us that our celebration would come to an end. When we reached camp, we quickly looked to unzip our tents for the warmth within, but the zipper on the fly to Mike and Guntis's tent was frozen shut. With their core temperatures plunging by the minute, they desperately punched out the clear plastic circular porthole on the outside tent flap and tumbled into the vestibule. They looked like the Keystone Cops. Within minutes, we were cutting bricks of ice with a wood-handled saw, after which we melted them in our aluminum pots and prepared our freeze-dried dinners while we warmed up in our tents. Following nine hours on our feet, sleep came easy. We had summited Mount Vinson and made it back to camp safe. Despite several setbacks, we were even ahead of schedule. We could be home by the end of the week.

Mt Vinson Summit, 12-16-2018

100% summit and safe return to High Camp. Exquisitely beautiful. We can't wait to share the pics. Almost no wind and warm through the climb. But back at High Camp the wind is howling again. Crazy weather. No wonder why no one has built a five-star resort here.... We hope to make it to Base Camp by late tomorrow then it is waiting on the planes! Thanks for all the support! (Chris Warner)

Lesson 5: Honor Others.

Visiting Derreon at Inova Hospital after she completed radiation treatment drove me to keep my promise to honor her on the Mount Vinson summit. Acknowledging her effort, hardship, and bravery was as important as reaching that goal. We had a tough day climbing that mountain, but it was a small task in comparison to Derreon's fight for survival.

 ULSE
OXYGEN

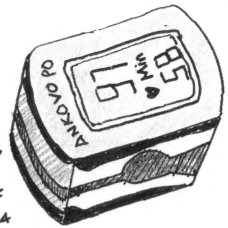

ON THE MOUNTAIN
WE MEASURE THE
PHYSICAL EFFECT of
ALTITUDE WITH A
"PULSE·OX" DEVICE THAT INDICATES HOW MUCH
OXYGEN IS IN YOUR BLOOD. 100% IS
TYPICAL AT SEA LEVEL. WHEN THE NUMBER
IS BELOW 75 YOU'RE IN DANGER.

- UNION GLACIER   IS AT ± 2,000 FT
- BASE CAMP.   7,021   ABOVE SEA
                                   LEVEL.
- LOW CAMP.   9,121
- HIGH CAMP.   12,402
- SUMMIT   16,050

·	12. 8	UNION GLACIER	95
·	12. 9	UNION GLACIER	90
·	12·10	UNION GLACIER	90
·	12.11	LOW CAMP.	78
·	12.12	LOW CAMP.	82
·	12.13	LOW CAMP.	88
	12.14	HIGH CAMP	82
·	12..15	HIGH CAMP	86
·	12.16	SUMMIT - HIGH CAMP	81
	12.17	BASECAMP.	87
	12.18	BASE CAMP	91

90] 7,000 FT
78] ELEVATION
     CHANGE
     IN 10 HOURS

CHAPTER SIX
DECEMBER 17

"Don't judge a book by its cover"
George Eliot (pen name for Mary Ann Evans)

WE AWOKE EARLY THE NEXT MORNING with one goal in mind: Get home in time for Christmas. That meant moving swiftly. We would have to reach Low Camp, gather our remaining gear, pack the sleds, and continue onward to reach Base Camp by the end of the day. Then, we could be first in line to fly to Union Glacier for hot showers, hot food, and a ticket on the transport back to civilization. We were dreaming of hotel rooms, restaurants, warm beds, the Internet, and Christmas Eve at home in a week.

Before we could leave, though, we would have to dig through six inches of frozen snow and ice that had covered the tent anchors. Three days of wind, cold, and drifting snow had buried the tent edges. We were eager to head out, but excavating our tent required patience. One wrong move and we could tear the nylon. The unrelenting winds of High Camp made the effort even more challenging. Our fingers numbed as we carefully wielded our ice axes. After an hour, the anchors finally emerged. Another hour and our packs were on our backs, our crampons were secured, and we clipped ourselves onto the rope line for the descent.

Although we were heading down, the return journey brought challenges the ascent hadn't. My pack was full, with 40 pounds of gear. I wrapped my right arm around the lead rope and slowly, deliberately descended, one boot after the other, making sure each crampon was anchored in the sloping ice before I took my next step. Halfway down, I looked at my feet in horror. The crampon on my left boot was dangling by its yellow strap. Below me, a dozen climbers were descending the ropes. If that crampon went free, it would topple, picking up speed as it tumbled, just as my water bottle had. If it followed the line of the rope, those sharp steel teeth could pierce a climber below like a spear.

I stopped and slowly bent down, trying to reach the crampon with one hand while holding the rope with the other, all the while balancing a loaded pack on my back. Before I could grab it, the crampon slid off my boot and shot down the rope line, barreling toward Guntis, who was clipping in below me. I prayed the crampon would spin away from the line. Instead, I watched in amazement as it miraculously came to a stop on a small snow-bank. I couldn't believe it. One moment it was tumbling end over end, gaining momentum. The next, it simply came to rest 30 feet below me, six feet beside the rope. With my remaining crampon securing one boot, I carefully lowered myself down, kicking my other boot into the ice slope for control. As I approached the crampon, I found myself facing a new problem. I was standing on a 40-degree slope covered in ice. How would I get the crampon safely on my boot?

Above me, a voice shouted out. "Don't worry, mate, I've got you covered." It was Andy, the lead guide from the Adventure Consultants team. After our run-in back at Union Glacier Camp

DAY NINE

9 HIGH CAMP, 12,402 ELEVATION, MT. V.

THE WINDS AT HIGH CAMP AS WE RETURNED
BACK FROM THE SUMMIT WERE FIERCE.
AS WE APPROACHED CAMP, THE TEMPS
DROPPED FROM 40°F TO -20F° WITHIN A
30 MIN TIME FRAME! BRRRRR.

SNOW
TENT

↕ 15" SNOW/ICE

THE DRIFTING SNOW AT HIGH CAMP BURIED
ALL OF OUR TENT ANCHORS...TOOK US 45 +
MINUTES TO JUST DIG OUT, BEFORE WE COULD
PACK UP OUR TENTS. FINALLY AT 11:00 AM
WE LEFT HIGH CAMP FOR BASE CAMP...A 7.4 MI
DESCENT.

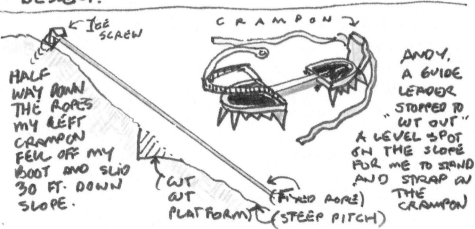

← ICE SCREW

CRAMPON ↘

HALF
WAY DOWN
THE ROPES
MY LEFT
CRAMPON
FELL OFF MY
BOOT AND SLID
30 FT. DOWN
SLOPE.

(CUT
OUT
PLATFORM)

(FIXED ROPE)
(STEEP PITCH)

ANDY,
A GUIDE
LEADER
STOPPED TO
"CUT OUT"
A LEVEL SPOT
ON THE SLOPE
FOR ME TO STAND
AND STRAP ON
THE
CRAMPON

over filling my water bottles, I wondered what he would say now.

Andy carefully descended the fixed rope and brought himself next to me. Reaching for his backpack, he unfastened his ice axe, asked me to take a few steps back and began chipping away at the icy slope. When he was done, he had chopped out a level pad about three feet in diameter in the steep slope. His teammate Glenn Hodges, who was tethered to Andy's rope line, had safely unclipped from the fixed rope to retrieve my crampon and had placed it near where Andy was standing.

"Stand here," Andy said as he reached for my crampon and handed it to me. "You should be good from here." Without another word, he continued down the ropes to his team.

I stood there in shock. That's when I saw that Andy had not only retrieved my crampon, but he had also reattached my tether to a safer location on the fixed rope without my knowledge. If he hadn't done so, I could have fallen 100 feet or more, right along the descending route, probably knocking over other climbers below me.

Andy was the last person on Mount Vinson I expected to help me out. How often do we form opinions of others based on snap judgments without fully understanding them? I realized that my disdain for Andy stemmed from an impetuous opinion formed in a few short moments back at Union Glacier Camp. I took solace in the decision to hold my tongue then. Amid this moment of terror, he taught me a valuable lesson about not jumping to conclusions about others.

Our team made it safely to the bottom of the ropes, and we arrived at Low Camp to find our gear and sleds covered with snow, but right where we had left them. In just 20 minutes, we loaded our gear onto the sleds and set out of camp. Only Andy's team was ahead of us. Home was calling.

As we set off for Base Camp, the crevasse fields and ice seracs shined in the bright afternoon sun, creating a scene even more spectacular than the one we had crossed on the climb. With lighter packs, an easier descent, and more oxygen surging into our lungs with each step, we were still glowing from having summited the day before, and we took in the icy world around us.

As we approached the first tents and storage buildings of the Base Camp entrance, we could see a small wooden table with a dozen fluted glasses and a *very* cold bottle of champagne, carefully arranged. How thoughtful of the camp manager to welcome us back. But then we realized, the champagne wasn't for us. It was for the ALE team. "Where is *our* champagne?" we asked Chris. He brushed us off.

We pulled our sleds to the spot next to the waterproof duffel bags that we'd buried in a cache a week ago and began the task of digging them out to establish our campsite on the ice. The journey had been fraught with peril, but we made it back safely. Chris once said that there are only three forms of conflict: Man versus nature, man versus man, and man versus himself. We experienced moments of all three of those, but overcoming the obstacles that nature put before us gave us our greatest sense of achievement. We had faced ice, wind, cold, crevasses, steep terrain, and knife-edge ridges and returned without injury. Chris's skillful leadership and our ability to work unselfishly as a team made the expedition a success.

Our only worries now were what to cook for dinner, when our flight to Union Glacier Camp would arrive, and when would we get home to celebrate Christmas with our families.

Mt Vinson Camp Two, 12-17-2018

The winds at High Camp as we returned from the summit were fierce. As we approached camp, the temps dropped from 30°F to –20°F in 30 minutes time frame! Brrr. The drifting snow at High Camp buried all our tent anchors... Took us 45+ minutes to just dig out before we could pick up our tents. Finally, at 11 AM we left High Camp for Base Camp. Shouldering our massive packs, we descended into the wind toward the 3,500 feet of fixed lines that lead us to the vast flat glacier. At the top of the glacier is "Low Camp." Here we loaded up the sleds and tracked across the ice for another 2.5 hours. We're now at Base Camp. The weather we've experienced for the past 10 days has been wreaking havoc on Antarctic flights. We need a day of clear skies to fly back to Union Glacier Camp where dozens of marathoners have been "trapped" because no flights from Punta Arenas have been able to fly to pick them up. We will be in the queue behind those folks. As if the high winds and crazy cold temps aren't enough! (Chris Warner)

Judah, age 10 – Knoxville, TN

Judah was the honoree on our descent from High Camp to Low Camp to Base Camp. He is battling a very rare form of brain cancer and being treated at St. Jude's Hospital. Hopecam connected him to his classmates during long visits to Memphis for treatment.

Mornings at Base Camp began with temperatures well below zero. Through the round porthole of our tent, I watched the sun arc upward from the horizon. By 9 a.m., it was warm enough to coax me out of the tent, crank up the stoves in our cook tent,

WE ARRIVED AT CAMP ONE AROUND 3AM
AND DUG OUT THE GEAR BAGS WE LEFT THERE.
AFTER PREPARING THE FOUR SLEDS WE
SET OUT FOR BASE CAMP IN PERFECT SUNSHINE
WITH VERY LITTLE WIND ... PASSING BY
MASSIVE ICE FALLS AND VAST STRETCHES
OF WIND SWEPT SNOW FIELDS. BY 7 PM WE
WERE SETTING UP OUR TENTS IN CAMP.

Mt
Vinson
Ice
Sculpture

P P P P P P P P P P
RUNWAY
P P P P P P P P P
ALE
BASE HQ
ALE
STORAGE
ALE
GUEST
TENTS
EXPEDITION
TENTS
DROP
OFF
PEE HOLE
TOILETS

BASE CAMP MAP. (OUR TENTS)

BASE CAMP MAP

DAY (10) 10

TUESDAY DECEMBER 18 2018
BASE CAMP, 7,021 ELEV.

THE MORNINGS ARE COLD AT BASE CAMP WITH TEMPERATURES AT OR BELOW ZERO AT 5:00 AM. BY 9:00 THE SUN WARMS UP AND ITS POSSIBLE TO START HEATING ICE FOR WATER FOR BREAKFAST.

THE FLIGHT COORDINATOR INFORMED US THAT AS SOON AS THE FOG AT BASE CAMP LIFTED, WE WOULD FLY BACK TO UNION GLACIER CAMP.....

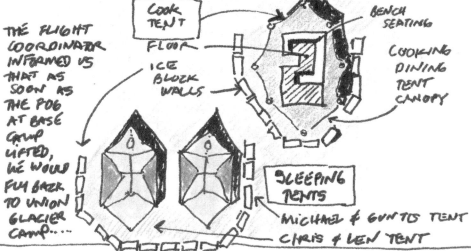

COOK TENT
FLOOR
ICE BLOCK WALLS
BENCH SEATING
COOKING DINING TENT CANOPY
SLEEPING TENTS
MICHAEL & GUNTIS TENT
CHRIS & LEN TENT

BUT AS BLUE SKIES EMERGED AT OUR LOCATION AT BASE CAMP, WE LEARNED THAT HIGH WINDS AT UNION GLACIER PREVENTED ALL FLIGHTS TUESDAY.

WE WERE TOLD TO PREPARE FOR HIGH WINDS AT BASE CAMP, SO WE BUILT 2½' TALL ICE BLOCK WALLS TO SURROUND OUR TENTS AND COOK TENT. WE HAD BEAN & EGG BURRITOS FOR BREAKFAST AND CHICKEN WITH PASTA FOR DINNER.

and start heating blocks of ice to make the hot water for coffee. At breakfast, our team was in a great mood, even though a fog had descended on Base Camp. We spoke to Fred Alldredge, the ski aircraft and safety coordinator. As soon as the fog lifted, he assured us, we would be on a twin-engine Otter back to Union Glacier Camp.

The skies turned bright and clear, but the plane never arrived. High winds, we learned, were buffeting Union Glacier. No flights would go out today.

> **Mt Vinson Base Camp, 12-18-2018**
> Waiting on planes seems to be an Antarctic theme. Luckily, we are ahead of schedule. Happily, the temps at Base Camp are a lot warmer than the upper camps, so we are anticipating a comfy night of hard-earned sleep. Everyone is healthy and happy. (Chris Warner)

Soon, the news grew even worse. The meteorologists at Union Glacier Camp were watching a storm system develop. High winds were bound for both Union Glacier and Base Camp. We had rushed down from High Camp, we realized, only to face the possibility of being stuck at Base Camp for days.

Making the best of a lousy situation, we set about making it our home. We fortified our site with three-foot-tall ice block walls to shelter our tents from whatever weather was coming. Antarctica offered plenty of such building materials, and we stacked the ice blocks into curved walls around each tent. Inside our cook tent, we built an ice bench and table.

After a breakfast of bean and egg burritos, the day passed quickly between naps and gear sorting. We packed our crampons, harnesses, and axes into heavy duffels outside our tent. We wouldn't need them anymore. We just needed an airplane to take us back.

> **Mt Vinson Camp Two, 12-18-2018**
> Welp! No flights today. Apparently, the winds at Union glacier are blowing too strong for the ski planes to take off... So, it was a long day of cooking meals and swapping stories with the other teams. The talk among the guides is that this was the worst weather anyone had experienced on Vinson. Crazy to think that in all the winds and extreme cold that there was so much summit success. Of the roughly 40+ climbers, all but six summited. The shared struggle has really bonded the climbers on the mountain. Even though we all need a shower there has been a lot of laughter in Base Camp. In the grand scheme of things, being "stuck" in such an exotic location is pretty cool. (Chris Warner)

Lesson 6: Don't judge others.

My first impression of Andy Cole was memorably negative, but I kept my criticisms to myself. My mother always told me as a child, "If you don't have anything nice to say about someone, don't say anything at all." Sound advice. The very person on the mountain I thought the least of ended up helping me at the time I needed it most. Reserving judgment, staying positive, and looking for the best in people holds true on the mountain and in life.

CHAPTER SEVEN
DECEMBER 18

"You have power over your mind—not outside events. Realize this, and you will find strength."

Marcus Aurelius

THE NEXT DAY, BASE CAMP was still socked in with fog. The situation was worse at Union Glacier, we heard. A windstorm pounded the camp, destroying several of the sturdy clamshell tents and leaving flights grounded. While we remained stuck at Base Camp, Union Glacier Camp was filling up with trapped adventurers either seeking to start their expeditions or head home.

Among them was a group of 60 runners who had competed in the Antarctic Ice Marathon. Each year, the race takes place on the perimeter of the ice runway where the prop planes arrive and depart. A little over four laps around the 10-kilometer course allows those who seek to complete a marathon on every continent to check Antarctica off their list. Five days after the marathon, they were still waiting for the weather to clear for the Ilyushin jet to depart Punta Arenas to pick them up. Their provisions were running low.

Ours were still holding up, but our frustration was growing.

With GPS-enabled navigation and one of the best weather fore-casting teams in the world, I felt, there had to be a way for planes to get to here safely. What would it take? Christmas was only a week away.

I set off to find Fred Alldredge in the small shelter where he worked next to the staff Quonset hut. Pilots didn't need sophisti-cated technology to gauge conditions in Antarctica, he explained. They just needed his eyes.

On a map, he pointed out to me six key landmarks that sur-rounded the camp. To the north and west were the three peaks along Boyce Ridge that sheltered our camp. To the south was a mountain called Penguin Point. To the east was a 500-foot rise flanked by crevasse fields that camp guides dubbed Ski Hill. At the foot of Mount Vinson was Branscombe Glacier. For the pilots to fly, he said, five of the six needed to be visible. Any less and they stayed on the ground.

Every three hours, Fred scored the visibility of each landmark and emailed the results to the weather forecasters at Union Glacier. A team of professional meteorologists worked around the clock there, providing twice-daily forecasts for the pilots and ground teams. In addition, ALE maintains dozens of solar-powered remote weather stations at strategic locations with webcams and anemom-eters providing real-time data throughout the continent. A "sea-space" satellite receiver produces high-resolution imagery to help the meteorologists predict weather patterns. For the planes to fly, conditions would need to be perfect.

The leaders of the climbing teams were nonchalant. They had experience in places like the Himalayas and the Andes, where vola-tile weather patterns dictated every movement. Many were former military, accustomed to a "hurry up and wait" schedule.

11

WEDNESDAY DECEMBER 19, 2018
BASE CAMP, 7,021 ELEV.

MORE FOG AND LOW VISIBILITY AT BASE
CAMP MADE IT IMPOSSIBLE FOR THE TWIN
OTTER PLANES TO FLY. ALSO HIGH WINDS
AT UNION GLACIER EXCEEDING 20 KNOTS CAUSED
ALL FLIGHTS TO BE GROUNDED. SEVERAL CLAM
SHELL TENTS WERE DESTROYED AT U.G.

TO PASS TIME, WE ARE GETTING TO KNOW
THE OTHER TEAMS AND THE CLIMBERS WHO
REACHED THE SUMMIT. MY NOSE WAS
SEVERELY WIND BURNED FROM THE CLIMB ON
THE ROPES - LOT OF BROWN BURNED SKIN AT
THE END OF MY NOSE. ALSO, I CHIPPED
A FRONT TOOTH ON SUMMIT DAY. TRYING
TO TIGHTEN A STRAP ON MY MITTEN. UGH!

SKI
HILL
ICE
FALL

BOYCE
RIDGE

VALLEY

BASE
CAMP
AREA

PENGUIN
POINT

RUNWAY

BOYCE
RIDGE

WEATHER REPORTS
ARE RADIOED IN
FROM BASE CAMP
TO UNION GLACIER
HOURLY W/ WIND
SPEED AND VISIBILITY
FROM (5) MOUNTAIN
TOPS

"It's all about your frame of reference," Mike Hamill, owner of Climbing the Seven Summits, told me. "After a hundred expeditions, you are mentally prepared for long logistical delays. You almost look forward to the freedom of having nothing to do." That wasn't necessarily true of his clients. "There are many Type-A personalities in this sport who have a difficult time surrendering control," he said. There were plenty of wealthy ones, too, but no amount of money would clear up the weather or get the planes off the ground.

"The down time is really a gift," Mike added, "that allows you to reflect, meet others, and find personal growth through books, writing in journals, and exploring the surroundings."

I didn't share his nonchalance. I was eager to get home. Still, I tried to make the best of being marooned in this stunning landscape. The only problem was, exploring the surroundings was dangerous. Outside camp were crevasse fields, steep slopes, and cliffs. I was stuck at a remote camp the size of a football field. If I had been marooned at Union Glacier Camp, hot showers and cold beer would have eased the agony. There were other activities to do there, including a marathon course to run. I had completed marathons in Europe, North America, and Asia. If I could get back to Union Glacier, I could get permission to run the groomed track and scratch the continent off my marathon bucket list. But first I had to get off the mountain.

Mt Vinson Camp Two, 12-19-2018

Welp! No flights today. We kept ourselves entertained by visiting others and cooking creative meals from an ever-dwindling supply of ingredients. Of course, this speculation about the weather conditions needed for the pilots fuels the rumor mills. Those of us who have waited for days in the mountain ranges on various continents have seen this before: Truth is you have no control and are happy that the pilots are conservative. Time to read another book. The planes will fly when it's safe... And the food... Antarctica is a great place to melt some belly fat and let the six-pack abs return. Funny bit of trivia: Seems every team is on a different time zone. We seem to be the early risers 6-7 AM Chile time. One group is making breakfast as we finish lunch. Others seem to sleep for 22 hours. I guess they eat brunch when awake. Twenty-Four hours of daylight plays crazy tricks on the body clock. (Chris Warner)

The day ended with more bad news. A rare storm dumped three feet of snow at Union Glacier Camp. Usually, Antarctica won't see more than six or eight inches of snow in a year. Some parts see none at all. To have three feet of snow in one storm was historic and astonishing. It would take days to plow the camp's two runways.

The massive Ilyushin jets, filled with food supplies, remained grounded in Punta Arenas. Camp chefs were cracking open reserve food supplies deep in storage to feed everyone. Worse yet, the camp was out of alcohol. Meanwhile, the ALE leadership team was juggling other problems. Dozens of ecotourists were stranded hundreds of miles away at the South Pole Camp. At Gould Bay, visitors who had come to see emperor penguins were running low on resources. Adventurers Colin O'Brady and Louis Rudd were within days of completing their cross-country ski race at the Ross Ice Shelf when the storm hit. After traversing almost 900 miles over 54 days while towing 330-pound sleds behind them, they were counting on ALE to pick them up at the end of their journey. Other expeditions also depended on them for logistical support. Rescuing our team, well rested and well fed, was influenced by many other priorities.

Despite a clear day at Base Camp, the fog below that covered the runway refused to clear. The six landmarks remained shrouded. At Union Glacier, we learned, plows were working furiously to clear the massive snowfall from the runways. Every able-bodied person in camp took up a shovel to help.

Here at Vinson, the expedition teams stayed occupied, too. Some were not faring well. As we sought solace with other adventurers, we befriended Tomas Ceppi, the Argentinian guide responsible for supporting the four-woman team. After 16 days, he had grown weary of cooking meals with a dwindling supply of ingredients, delivering them to his client's tents twice daily, and cleaning up when they were done. Tomas visited our tent often to trade food supplies and spin tales with our team.

Other teams coped with the boredom by building an ice block Christmas tree 14 feet high, with red and green climbing rope strung like lights. Below, they wrapped ropes around ice blocks like ribbon on Christmas presents under the tree. It looked like Santa had traveled from the North Pole to the south to surprise us, though someone surely would have spotted him. There were no landings in camp and no nights in a polar summer.

Mike Hamill had brought a Nerf football, and we spent an hour passing the ball with his team. On the other side of camp,

THE FLIGHT COORDINATOR BROUGHT MORE BAD NEWS. UNION GLACIER WAS DUMPED WITH 3" OF SNOW OVERNIGHT. A RECORD AMOUNT. THE ENTIRE CONTINENT AVERAGES 4" OF SNOW PER YEAR! ALL THE RUNWAYS AT UNION GLACIER NEED TO BE PLOWED FOR ANY FLIGHTS TO REPORT. MEANWHILE HERE AT BASE CAMP WE HAD A SUNNY DAY WITH LIGHT FOG IN THE VALLEY WHERE THE PLANES APPROACH THE LANDING STRIP.

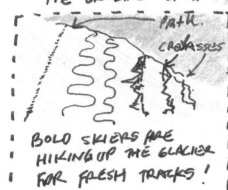

PATH. CROASSES

BOLD SKIERS ARE HIKING UP THE GLACIER FOR FRESH TRACKS!

SNOW BLOCK XMAS — TREES —

Ribbon "gift wrap" on ice blocks

AT THIS RATE WE WILL NEED TO START GIFT WRAPPING OUR "GU" PACKETS FOR A XMAS EVE PARTY TO CELEBRATE WITH THE 40+ FOLKS STUCK HERE!

the ALE team built an igloo to pass the time. When Fred showed up, he was the bearer of more bad news. All flights would be grounded until after the 25th. Our last hope of making it home for Christmas vanished.

I would need to call my family, and I was dreading it. I had never missed a Christmas with my wife, Elizabeth, and our kids, Matt and Viena. I felt selfish. I knew when I agreed to this expedition that we could face delays—its harsh altitudes and latitudes could be unpredictable—but the likelihood of missing Christmas Day seemed remote. Now, I felt like I had put this climb ahead of my family.

It was a complaint I was sensitive to. I started endurance training when Matt had cancer, and I was spending at least 25 hours a week on it, in addition to running my own business. Once, when Viena was 13, she pulled me aside as I was preparing for a multi-day bike race. When her grade school friends had visited for sleepovers, she told me, I used to cook them pancakes for breakfast. Now, I'm out training. And after dinner when she would need help with her homework, I was asleep on the couch. "Dad," she said, "I know you're racing for a good reason, but as a father you've really not been there for me."

After the bike race was over, I repaid my family for those long absences while training. I was more present, supportive, and engaged—and I cooked a lot of pancakes and fried a lot of bacon for my daughter on weekend mornings. Now, I was stuck in Antarctica for Christmas. Pancakes and bacon wouldn't cut it.

Guntis had brought a satellite phone to Base Camp, with pre-purchased talk time. He graciously loaned me the phone, and I promised to keep my call to 10 minutes. I pulled off my heavy gloves to dial, then quickly put them back on as I walked the camp perimeter hoping for some privacy. When they answered, I told them the news. Everyone was understanding.

"Just come back," Viena said. She sounded nervous but encouraging. "We will wait to have Christmas with you."

It was exactly what I needed to hear.

Mt Vinson Base Camp, 12-20-2018

Over the last 24 hours a meter of snow has fallen at Union Glacier Base Camp. This is the airstrip where the twin Otter planes with skis are based. It is also where the jet from Chile lands on the blue ice runway. Until the storm stops at UG we are stuck at Vinson Base Camp. It is anyone's guess as to when the planes can fly. Luckily at Vinson Base Camp the sun is shining, and the winds are mild. We still have plenty of food and spirits are high. Lots of talk this morning about the need to remain optimistic.

(8 hours later) No planes could fly today. Fingers are crossed that tomorrow sees an improvement. We are working on changing flight dates to come back home. We will keep you posted. Spirits remain high and some food trading has spiced our culinary options. (Chris Warner)

Another problem was beginning to develop. After taking inventory of our supplies, we realized we had enough food to sustain us for about five more days and no idea how much longer we might be stuck here. We had consumed the last pasta dish in our provisions. The coffee, sugar, and cookies were all gone. Our team had prepared for two weeks on the ice. This was day 10. If we rationed what remained and eliminated lunch, we figured, maybe we could stretch our supplies to last another week.

When the camp leader learned of our dwindling supplies, he ducked into ALE's underground storage locker and emerged with a two-pound bag of hash browns, three pounds of bacon bits, and a pound of coffee. Breakfast the next morning felt like brunch at the Ritz-Carlton, but it came with a warning. Another storm was coming, and it was heading directly for our camp.

Lesson 7: Focus on what you can control.

Stuck at Base Camp, I had to accept the circumstances of my situation and adapt accordingly. Everything in life falls into two buckets: What you can control, and what you cannot. The best outcome was accepting my fate and making the best of a difficult situation with the hope that things will improve.

CHAPTER EIGHT
DECEMBER 20

"I can tell you who didn't make it out, it was the optimists."
*Admiral James Stockdale, survivor of seven years of imprisonment at the
Vietnam war camp dubbed "The Hanoi Hilton"*

WITH THE STORM HOURS AWAY from striking camp, Chris and
I broke out the saw and began cutting large ice blocks and stack-
ing them to completely enclose the tents. Around the cook tent, we
built a second layer wall higher than the first. Our cooking area
looked so secure, we dubbed it "the Lifeboat."

Exhausted, I sat atop my sleeping bag, stripped off my wet clothes, and stuffed them into the bag so my body temperature could help dry them while I slept. But sleep didn't come easy. At 4 a.m., I woke to gusting winds pummeling the top of the tent. Since our arrival, fierce winds had blown from the top of Branscombe Ridge, so we positioned the opening of our tents on the leeward side. This storm was blowing from the opposite direction.

The ice block walls we built were doing their job, though, and our tents remained intact, with us safe inside. I unzipped the tent fly to peek out through the open window. The plastic panel that once lined the window had come unglued at High Camp, but it allowed a clear view out the opening. Guntis and Mike's tent had the same problem, except they had purposefully busted the window at High Camp.

Our tents had come to mirror those of us who inhabited them. We were among the camp elders—the gray-haired ones who had been to the summit and back and learned valuable lessons about the world and ourselves along the way. Our tents were old, tattered, and tearing at the seams, but like us, they were holding together. Other teams were watching us, gauging our reaction to the circumstances. We were the only climbers who did not pay an expedition guide service to bring them here. We were an independent, hand-picked team, and through hardship after hardship, we endured.

My two-liter pee bottle was full, and I'd need to empty it. But such an errand meant braving the wind and cold. I dressed quietly, trying not to wake Chris, and I unzipped the tent flap and crawled backward into the vestibule. Bottle in hand, I crossed the 100 feet to the pee hole marked by a yellow flag. Winds were blowing at 30 knots, snapping the camp flag straight. For

DAY **13**
BASE CAMP
EL. 7021 FT.

FRIDAY DECEMBER 21, 2018

DAY 5 OF THE BASE CAMP SIEGE

WOKE UP THIS MORNING TO A
MAJOR WIND STORM BLOWING
20-30 KNOTS CREATING A "WHITE
OUT" THE STORM LASTED THE
ENTIRE DAY DRIVING TEMPS TO
-20 WITH THE WINDCHILL.

solar panel

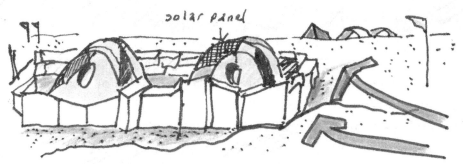

CHRIS AND I CUT SOME LARGER ICE BLOCKS
TO STOP THE WIND BLOWING FROM 'UP VALLEY'
WE STACKED THEM LIKE DOMINOES ... WORKED
WELL. CHRIS BROUGHT A
FIRST RATE SOLAR PANEL
ELECTRICAL CHARGER
THAT FORTUNATELY
DID NOT BLOW OFF
THE ROOF OF THE
TENT DURING THE STORM.

36"

48"

BRUNTON

a moment, it felt like I was back amid the gusts at High Camp. These gales are called katabatic winds. They sporadically plunge down the face of the mountains at hurricane speed and strike with ferocious power. I took one last look around and then hurried back to warmth of my tent.

Later, we cooked breakfast in the Lifeboat, donning our warmest mittens to save our fingers from frostbite while trying to keep the mittens from catching on fire from the stove. When we finished, the winds receded enough to allow us walk around camp and check in with the other climbers. When I ran into Andy, I saw he needed help. After he had rescued my runaway crampon, it was the least I could do.

His team, the Adventure Consultants, had one of the largest cook tents in camp. The warmth from the nonstop solar radiation had melted the once-level areas inside the tent for seating and cooking. When a new team arrived, they would find a warped and tilted space inside. I helped his team dig out the dozen anchors, packed under two feet of snow. We then lifted the tent and moved it 20 feet away to a clear section of ice. We excavated a new trench four feet deep to create a level cooking and seating area in the ice. It was the best workout I'd had since we'd descended from High Camp earlier in the week. It felt great. So did the Scotch that Andy had stashed in his supply bin that he shared with my teammates and me after dinner.

Not knowing how long we would be confined at Base Camp was wearing on us. "Today is the day that the planes will come. I just know it," Mike said one morning. I was wary of his optimism.

BRUTAL, WINDY & BITTER DAY. WE SPENT THE ENTIRE DAY STAVING OFF FROSTBITE IN THE SLEEP TENTS & COOK TENTS. THE ALE STRUCTURES ARE "OFF LIMITS" FOR 'NON-ALE' GROUPS

WE SPENT ALL OF OUR TIME OUTSIDE OF OUR SLEEP TENTS IN THE COOK TENT. HERE'S A DIAGRAM OF THE INTERIOR

OUR "DOTARD" COOK TENT

① Cheese & crackers
② Can of mushrooms
③ Guntis coffee cup
④ Hot water pot
⑤ Aluminum pot
⑥ 1en Nalgene bottle
⑦ Garbage bag

⑧ Cooking stove
⑨ Pole holding up tent
⑩ Ice Block holding up tent
⑪ Center pier
⑫ Cutting knife
⑬ Guntis. S.
⑭ Chris W.

TONIGHT'S DINNER WAS PHILLY CHEESE STEAK SANDWICHES MADE WITH ONIONS, MUSHROOMS CHEESE & CHICKEN SLICES SERVED ON BUNS

Mt Vinson Base Camp, 12-21-2018
Woke up to high winds, blowing snow and cold temps. Looks like another day stuck in the tents. We may be running low on coffee, but the dumb jokes and witty conversations are to be found in excess. A true reinforcement of the saying "who you climb with is more important than what you climb!" (Chris Warner)

I remembered something I had heard Admiral James Stockdale say about his seven years in the brutal prisoner-of-war camp during the Vietnam War that came to be known as the Hanoi Hilton:

"The optimists, they were the ones who said, 'We're going to be home by Christmas.' Christmas would come, and it would go. And there would be another Christmas and they died of a broken heart."

Of course, we weren't prisoners of war, but we were marooned with no idea when we would get out. As each day's hope faded, I feared Mike would spiral into depression. I decided to set my reference point for leaving camp at mid-January. If the planes came earlier, I'd be elated. Otherwise, I was prepared to make Base Camp my home for weeks.

I took a tip from Laurence Gonzales and his book *Deep Survival: Who Lives, Who Dies, and Why.* In dire situations, Gonzales wrote, it's important to observe your situation, focus on small tasks, and take pleasure in completing them. Observing my situation was easy. We may die of boredom, but starvation was nowhere on the horizon. The underground cooler had more stashes of food if we needed them, and if things grew even more desperate, we could climb to Low Camp and High Camp for emergency supplies stashed there. In the meantime, teams bartered to diversify their menus, swapping extra coffee for a helping of sausages. I joked about hoarding the salt. We tried to laugh, taking bets on who we would have to sacrifice to help the tribe.

Mt Vinson Base Camp, 12-21-2018
Another day of no flights. There have been clouds obscuring the runway which is tucked in between several mountains. All we can do is continue to hope for a change in the weather patterns. Maybe tomorrow? A trough of bad weather continues to accumulate. At Union Glacier camp, there are 198 people waiting to fly home, but the blowing snow has reduced visibility to 200 yards, grounding the planes. There is a faint glimmer of hope that planes will fly on Christmas! (Chris Warner)

Focusing on small tasks wasn't hard, either. Helping Andy's team dig their tent felt good. I imagined being back home in Virginia. *What would I wish I had done during my confinement? What would I regret?* I remembered a time when I was in my mid-twenties, and I faced a similar situation.

• • • • •

Recently married, I got an opportunity to work in Saudi Arabia. I had earned a degree in landscape architecture and joined an international design firm with large projects in the Middle East. Senior managers were recruiting a landscape architect to help redevelop the old Riyadh airport property into King Salman Park. It was a one-year assignment that would pay double what I was earning, with all living expenses included and a two-week vacation every two months. Elizabeth would be able to join me in three months. We looked at it as an opportunity to travel the world, experience a new culture, and save enough money to buy a house when we returned. I agreed to take the job. A month later, I was flying business class on Saudia airlines for the 15-hour flight from New York to Riyadh.

After just 10 weeks, though, before Elizabeth could join me, the project abruptly ended. I was eager to get home, but I needed an exit visa. The engineering firm submitted the necessary forms, but after a week, I still hadn't heard any news. Every morning, I borrowed the company car and drove to check on the visa. Around me, dozens of foreign workers shouted in Arabic, clamoring for their passports. A young clerk sat at a desk with hundreds of passports arranged in tall stacks. He took one from the top of the stack and shouted out a name. If no one came forward, he set it on top of another stack and called out the next one.

When I reached the front of the line and got the clerk's attention, I asked about my exit visa. "*Inshallah*," he said. God willing.

After five trips, I grew despondent.

Two weeks later, I managed to get an appointment with the company's founder to see if he could help me. I was escorted into an office that looked like a museum gallery. The sofa and chairs would have fit in at Versailles. Old tapestries and paintings framed in gold adorned the walls. The doors opened and a tall, elderly man with a gray beard greeted me. He wore a traditional head scarf—a *keffiyeh*—a long, white, gold-trimmed robe, and a very expensive-looking pair of shoes.

"Please sit down," he said as he gestured to the sofa. Slowly, he poured me a cup of tea from a sterling silver pot and offered sugar and milk.

"Tell me about your experience in my beautiful country," he said. "What have you seen? What have you learned?"

It had been a wonderful experience, I told him. I had camped one weekend in the desert, visited historic sites in the countryside, toured modern architecture in the capital, and met lots of interesting people from Saudi Arabia and around the world. But, I said, "After waiting idly for two weeks for the exit visa, I just want to go home."

He looked at me calmly. "Why be so impatient?" he asked. "This likely will be your only opportunity to visit Saudi Arabia. This time is a gift that could be used to experience our people and culture." As I left his office, I thanked him for the meeting. "Your visa will be ready tomorrow," he said.

• • • • •

Marooned on the ice at Base Camp, I thought of that man in the desert. He was right. Time was a gift.

Christmas Eve arrived. Santa did not appear in a twin-engine ski plane, dashing the dreams of 37 mountaineers, but as a community we spent the evening wishing one another a Merry Christmas. Guntis let me use his satellite phone to call Elizabeth, Viena, and Matt, who were following the family Christmas tradition of dining at a Thai restaurant near our home. In my own way, I was joining them. Our team's Christmas Eve dinner was freeze-dried pad Thai.

Christmas Day was bright and warm enough for a light fleece jacket. The climbers gathered for a team picture in front of our ice block Christmas tree, with multicolored carabiners added to adorn the red and green climbing ropes. With an ample supply of colored pencils, paper, and a pair of scissors, I contributed colorful paper snowflakes to the tree. Chris joined in, too. We laughed. It reminded us of arts and crafts project in Catholic school.

It also served as a reminder of how much Chris and I had in common. We had both gone to parochial school and served as altar boys at early morning church masses. We had paper routes, bagged groceries, and held a dozen different jobs before our 16th birthdays. We hustled for spending money. Neither of our parents paid allowances. We were raised in hard-working middle-class suburban communities—I in suburban Cleveland and Chris in North Jersey. If we

By far not the typical christmas eve, but we made the most of the day celebrating together sharing it with new friends.

DAY 16; 6th DECEMBER 24th 2018 (BASE CAMP)

Christmas Eve

Most notable is that we are about as far from santa's workshop since we are 500 miles away from the SOUTH POLE

THE WHITEST CHRISTMAS EVER!

Christmas Eve in Base Camp was sunny and warm as the entire group of **40+** mountain climbers gathered together for a team picture in front of an 8' tall snow christmas tree!

mt Vinson snow sign

climbing ropes (red and green)

snow tree

paper snow flakes by len + chris

CHRISTMAS DAY 2018

VINSON BASE CAMP, ANTARCTICA.

DAY 17

SANTA DID NOT COME TO BASE CAMP LAST NIGHT AND MAKE THE DREAMS OF 40 MOUNTAINEERS COME TRUE APPEARING IN A TWIN ENGINE OTTER ... BUT AS A TEAM AND A COMMUNITY WE SPENT THE DAY WISHING ONE ANOTHER A MERRY CHRISTMAS.

I WAS ABLE TO SPEAK WITH ELIZABETH, VIENA AND MATT THANKS TO GUNTIS' IRIDIUM SATELLITE PHONE. CHRISTMAS EVE DINNER WAS HELD AT A THAI RESTAURANT IN FALLS CHURCH, VA FOR MY FAMILY. IRONICALLY OUR TEAM HAD CHICKEN PAD THAI FOR DINNER! ONLY OURS WAS FREEZE DRIED, PREPARED BY ADDING WATER TO A BAG!

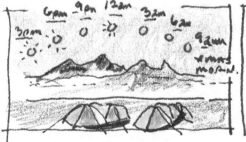

THERE WAS NO CHRISTMAS "EVE" BECAUSE THERE WAS NO DARKNESS ON DEC. 24th IN ANTARCTICA.

AFTER DINNER, THE ALE LEADERS BROUGHT PUDDING OVER TO THE ADVENTURE CONSULTANTS TENT WHERE WE WERE SHARING THE NIGHT.

wanted money, we had to find a job and earn it. We grew up in families with fathers who saved up for a one-week family beach vacation each year. We earned college degrees, launched successful businesses, and earned enough to travel the world and share this adventure in Antarctica. We proudly attached our paper ornaments on the ice tree.

Mt Vinson Base Camp, 12-24-2018

The cook tent is like a teepee with no floor and a center pole. We've carved out the floor to build the narrow benches and a cook surface. The hallway is 2 feet wide. Passing takes care to not knock over the center pole or nudge your neighbor. With four of us it is cramped cold and moist. The person closest to the stove is the cook and the guy closest to the door is the garbage man. Each of us has a talent: cleaning, cooking, or offering opinions. We call our little cook tent "the lifeboat." Only thing missing are the sharks. The team is very careful with our emotions. It would be easy to give into pessimism and all the emotions are contagious. Antarctica is giving a real chance to practice gratitude and optimism. Just saw the forecast and Santa is trying to bring a weather window on Christmas. Chance of flights is currently predicted at 70%-80% on Christmas afternoon. Teams are sharing food and the Germans carved a beautiful Madonna and child from a block of snow. Michelangelo would approve. Update 8:20 PM. For lunch we had dried hash browns with garlic, salt, pepper, ketchup, and Tabasco, topped with bacon crumbles. We chased it down with chicken noodle soup. By the time lunch was slurped up the ice crept into our tent, so it is now back to the tent to read, draw or retell dumb stories. Day 8 is passing as slowly as day 3 did.

Mt Vinson Base Camp, 12-25-2018

Merry Christmas!!! Send Rudolph!!! We woke up to a fog bank obscuring Vincent Basecamp. Visibility is maybe 100 meters, maybe. No word yet if there is a clearing at U.G. Like dutiful penguins we will sit tight. As always, we are keeping each other's spirits high! We are all blessed with being optimists.

Len has us making paper snowflakes and a big group of people just built a Christmas tree of snow. Everyone is gathering for a picture! We do all miss our families and are extremely grateful for their love. Santa came to the Christmas tree decorating. We hung Len's snowflake cut-outs on the tree. Weather is getting better. Hoping for showers for Christmas. Some good news: the Ilyushin jet is in the air flying from Punta Arenas, Chile, to U.G. with over 150 waiting there and a lack of food. It is great the system is working again. No flights to Base Camp today because of the fog, which has blocked the sun. Aboard the lifeboat, the scruffy bearded crew ate spaghetti with pesto for dinner while the Vince Guaraldi Trio soundtrack from the "Charlie Brown's Christmas" played in the background. If anyone has pull, send Rudolph! Guiding a sleigh in Antarctica would be a great resume builder for him. Ho Ho Ho from the South Pole! (Chris Warner)

Celebrating Christmas was a nice reprieve from the drudgery of camp life and a pleasant distraction from the *Groundhog Day* sameness it offered. The camp staff dressed up as elves. The chef wore a Santa costume and rode around camp on a yellow plastic sled pulled by a staff member with a plastic horse head—a stand-in for a reindeer. The camp director walked from tent to tent, passing around paper plates with servings of banana cream pie. As we ate dinner in our cook tent, I played music from *A Charlie Brown Christmas* on my iPhone. It was my favorite Christmas album. I would have preferred to be listening to it with my family, but here at camp, I found our common hardship was forging an indelible bond amid our community of climbers. Sitting on a block of ice, under a nylon tarp 600 miles from the South Pole, I felt at peace.

Lesson 8: Change your frame of reference.

Our circumstances do not determine whether we will experience hope or despair. It's our mind that decides. Stuck in Saudi Arabia, I realized I missed an opportunity to gain a deeper insight to people very different from me. We would miss Christmas with our families, but there was hope we would celebrate the New Year. Many thought we would be home in days. I was prepared for weeks. If the planes came in sooner, that would be a nice surprise.

CHAPTER NINE
DECEMBER 26

"The summit is what drives us,
but the climb itself is what matters."
Conrad Anker, renowned rock climber, mountaineer, and author

CHRISTMAS CAME AND WENT with feelings of relief and hope. We were growing anxious to leave, but each day taught us not to get too hopeful.

I woke up hungry and while my teammates slept, I fired up the stove to make myself a bowl of instant oatmeal. It was a deliberately selfish act. Our team worked as a unit. We moved at the same time, divided chores evenly, and always shared meals. We each had a private stash of favorite snacks, but the food in the duffel bags belonged to the team. As I finished the last spoonful and began cleaning up, I sorted through the duffel bag filled with the last of our food provisions. Where was the rest of the oatmeal? I knew we had packed another box, but it was nowhere to be found. I had just eaten our last ration. When the team joined me in the Lifeboat, I confessed. They laughed it off, but I could tell Mike was annoyed. Our food supply was dwindling.

So was our patience. This was our eighth day in isolation, and

DAY 18

WEDNESDAY DECEMBER 26th 2018
MT. VINSON BASECAMP. ELEV. 7021
DAY 10 OF THE "SIEGE AT MT VINSON"

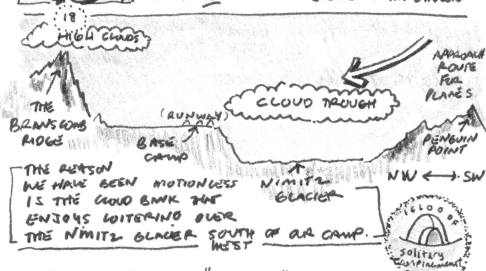

18 HIGH CLOUDS

THE BRANSCOMB RIDGE

(RUNWAY)

BASE CAMP

CLOUD TROUGH

APPROACH ROUTE FOR PLANES

PENGUIN POINT

NIMITZ GLACIER

NW ⟵⟶ SW

THE REASON WE HAVE BEEN MOTIONLESS IS THE CLOUD BANK THAT ENJOYS LOITERING OVER THE NIMITZ GLACIER SOUTH WEST OF OUR CAMP.

IGLOO OF solitary confinement

TODAY I OFFICIALLY "CRACKED" AND MISTAKENLY ATE OUR LAST RATION OF OATMEAL WITHOUT ASKING PERMISSION FROM THE LIFEBOAT CREW. (F HONESTLY THOUGHT WE HAD ANOTHER BAG IN THE BLUE SUPPLY BAG) F WAS DUTIFULLY REPRIMANDED BY BEING DENIED A TASTE OF THE HASH BROWNS WITH BACON BITS FROM COSTCO. THAT WERE PREPARED BY THE LIFEBOAT CHEFS ....

AS PENANCE I DID FOUR (4) LOOPS ON THE 1/4 MILE SNOW TRACK DOING SQUATS WITH A 20 LB ICE BLOCK

ICE BLOCK →

QUAKER OATS

ANTARCTIC CROSSFIT WORKOUT

the mental stress fractures were showing. A supreme court judge from the Czech Republic began pacing the quarter-mile perimeter path around the camp for hours every day without speaking, clasping his hands behind his back. When I first met him after the summit, he was jovial and engaging, but he was becoming more withdrawn and introspective as the days wore on.

While the increased risk of frostbite was a growing fear, food insecurity topped our concerns. Some began to complain that the ALE team gave priority to South Pole tourists over us. A contingent of grumblers grew amongst the camp inhabitants. Emotions are contagious, and I found myself joining them. ALE *could* be doing more to help us, I complained to Guntis. Chris quickly pulled me aside and told me to shelve the negativity.

"You're one of the most positive people I know," he said. "People are watching you. If you start complaining it will spread." He was right. The stress of uncertainty was affecting me. I heeded his advice and kept my complaints quiet.

Chris coped with the solitude by listening to podcasts. Guntis and I talked about cycling in Italy and Switzerland. Mike chatted up newfound friends in other camps. The Saudi gentleman from 30 years earlier had it right. This delay should be an opportunity, not a burden. It was an opportunity to get to know fellow mountaineers, share experiences, and appreciate the majesty of the mountains and glaciers in every direction that I would likely never see again.

Nine days without exercise was taking its toll on me, though. At home, I worked out every day, but here, with our food supplies almost gone, I didn't want to build up a hunger by exercising. I needed to do something to keep my sanity, though. Heading out to the perimeter, I thought I'd try some CrossFit, Antarctica style. I set out to walk around the pathway surrounding the camp perimeter, carrying a block of ice over my head and executing lunges on alternating steps for good measure. I figured the folks back at Parable Fitness in Virginia would get a laugh out of my Antarctic workout, so I recruited a fellow climber to shoot video on my phone.

Her name was Emily Farkas, a climber with the Seven Summits team. We had laughed at the coincidence of our shared last name. It's hard to find another Farkas. On my family's side, Forkas was the result of a hospital clerk's misspelling when my father was born. What were the chances of finding two Farkases in Antarctica?

Emily was an avid mountaineer, adventurer, and expedition doctor who lived in Davenport, Iowa. An accomplished cardiothoracic surgeon, she spent her career balancing her time between surgery in Iowa and volunteering to serve poor patients around the world. An honorary fellow of the organization World Extreme Medicine, she has directed and participated in more than 35 missions around the world.

Emily introduced me to two other climbers on her team—Mrika and Arianit Nikqi, from Peja, Kosovo. Mrika was seeking to become the youngest woman in the world to climb the Seven Summits. She had summited Kilimanjaro the previous summer. Vinson would be her second. She hoped to reach the goal before her 18th birthday, but as a 17-year-old high school senior, she had a seemingly impossible schedule ahead of her.

Arianit, her father, was a successful corporate attorney and an accomplished mountaineer. He had introduced his daughter to climbing when she was just seven, and it became a shared passion for them. By the time Mrika was a teenager, Arianit had introduced her to some of the most challenging peaks in the Alps. I admired the close relationship this father-daughter team shared and the maturity, tenacity, and athletic ability of such a young person from a part of the world I knew so little about. And I am happy to report Mrika accomplished her goal in 2019 after summiting the Carstensz Pyramid in Indonesia at the age of 17.

I came to enjoy meeting the other mountaineers—driven, passionate adventurers who came here from around the world and found themselves stuck in Antarctica, just like me. I met Bouchra Baibanou. She had just completed a TEDx Casablanca talk before coming here. With Vinson, she had become the first Moroccan mountaineer to conquer the Seven Summits. Brad Watts came from Perth, Australia, and we found we shared a common interest in childhood cancer. In 2015, Brad's two-year-old daughter was diagnosed with brain cancer. She survived, and Brad, a successful energy executive, raises funds for nonprofits that support families of children fighting cancer in his community. But my greatest surprise was getting to know Andy Cole, the guide who helped me with my lost crampon on the Vinson headwall. Andy was not the know-it-all I first thought he was. Not just an accomplished mountaineer, he had a deep love and respect for this continent we found ourselves trapped on. Andy supported wildlife research in Antarctica and worked with a team studying the diet and habitat of emperor penguins. In minute detail, he could describe how many scientists it takes to tackle a penguin and subdue and probe it for a fecal sample. We laughed. I was glad it wasn't my line of work.

What struck me about all these people was their attitude. Instead of feeling trapped in an ice prison, they made the most of their time here. We opened up to each other, built new relationships, and shared a sense of curiosity toward one another that could outlast our time here at Base Camp.

The Germans, however, were more withdrawn despite our effort to engage with them. I could not imagine their frustration, having been the only team not to have reached the summit. The logistical costs of simply getting to and from Antarctica make Mount Vinson one of the most expensive expeditions in the world, and it must have been painful to be surrounded by other mountaineers sharing summit-day photographs.

Mt Vinson Base Camp 12-26-2018
Fog crept upon camp at breakfast and stuck to our minds and souls like peanut butter to the roof of your mouth. No planes can fly from U.G. leaving us to spend another day wondering about the origin of body odor, the meaning of life and seeking the exact moment when humor feeds into apathy. All philosophizing aside, I'm reading "Man's Search for Meaning," the brilliant book by Holocaust survivor and psychologist Victor Frankl. It is the perfect book for a week spent in a tent. His ability to learn from suffering is best appreciated in our contemplative environment, where I can stop on every page and talk through the lesson with a tent mate. I have vowed to write the sequel — "Man's Search for Cleaning" – the redemptive powers of soap and water (hot). Any prophet returning from Antarctica will need to shower before others will embrace them. At this moment we smell more like fishmongers then philosophers. Day 10 will slowly become day 11 giving us the boundless enthusiasm and unbridled joy needed to fuel our results. (Chris Warner)

As the temperature warmed each afternoon, we noticed that our Lifeboat was starting to sag. The dugout walls were melting, like the tent from Andy Cole's team that I helped clean up. The metal post supporting the tent was loosening. It was time to execute a major kitchen renovation, we decided. We took the tent apart and, with shovels and saws, reconstructed the excavation. Like most home improvement projects, we added a few new items. We gave ourselves wider benches. We enlarged the cooking surface. We even added a few custom-built storage areas, all with shovels, saws, and knives. We set up the tent canopy over the newly improved space, secured the anchors, and celebrated over lunch. Minor tasks like these helped ease the difficulties of being marooned here. They gave us something to look forward to, and they helped make these ice walls our home for a while. Not knowing when a plane might arrive, we could make the most of where we were in the meantime.

I awoke at 4 a.m. the next morning, unzipped the tent, and peered out of the hole in our tent's vestibule at the landscape lit by the low morning sun. In the distance, I saw the nose of Penguin Point rising above the ice sheet. I hadn't seen it in days. I remembered Fred's daily Base Camp weather reports to Union Glacier. To fly, the pilots needed clear sight of five of the six landmarks. Penguin Point was one, clear as ever, rising to the south of the camp.

I stepped out of the tent to the designated pee hole and spun around to check the other landmarks. There was Branscombe Glacier rising toward Vinson. There was Ski Hill. There were the three peaks of Boyce Ridge. All were sharp and clear. The fog had lifted. The storm had subsided. We knew the Ilyushin already had made it from Punta Arenas to Union Glacier's blue ice runway. We just needed the Otter to be able to reach Base Camp enough times to ferry 37 stranded mountaineers home. I gave myself permission to be optimistic. We would be flying home today. I knew it.

I climbed back into my sleeping bag barely able to suppress my smile as I burrowed in. The entire camp was asleep, the air too cold to venture out or start the stove to make coffee. By 9 a.m. the sun was high enough to warm the air, allowing us to venture to the Lifeboat to start the stoves. Within an hour, the rest of the crew was up and about, prepping whatever was left of our breakfast provisions. I had to hope the plane would come today. Our food supplies were almost gone. We had a few helpings of bacon, cheese, and hash browns for breakfast. After that, just three freeze-dried packs of Thai chicken remained.

"Good news, boys!" said Fred as he zipped open the Lifeboat fly and popped in. "The Otters are flying today! You're on the second flight out!"

"Finally!" Guntis said.

Smiles spread quickly across all our faces within seconds of Fred's announcement. It wasn't just good news. It was great news. But we'd have to move quickly. With dreams of warm beds and cold beers, we started breaking down the camp and packing up our gear to haul it all to the runway.

By midmorning, the drone of twin engines hummed up the valley. The speck of the Otter grew as it neared and made its first landing at Base Camp in over two weeks. Our group of castaway climbers lined the runway, cheering and applauding as it touched down, kicking up a cloud of snow. The plane spun around, and the passengers disembarked. The next rotation of climbers had been waiting over a week at Union Glacier Camp. They quickly unloaded their colorful duffel bags full of the gear they would need to climb Vinson.

"Rookies," we whispered. They couldn't wait to arrive, and we couldn't wait to leave. We felt like grizzled, battle-hardened soldiers watching fresh-faced replacements march past. In 10 minutes, the plane was loaded with the first round of climbers, and it taxied to the runway. The small black flags marking the edges of the runway fluttered as the pilot eased down the throttle and the dron-

THURSDAY DECEMBER 27th 2018

DAY 19
BASE CAMP
TO
UNION GLACIER

THE SIEGE AT BASE CAMP IS OVER!

FINALLY AFTER BEING TRAPPED FOR TEN DAYS AT BASE CAMP THE WEATHER FINALLY CLEARED AND WE ESCAPED ON THE TWIN OTTER AT NOON TIME.

DEPARTING VINSON BASE CAMP 12:50 PM THURSDAY.

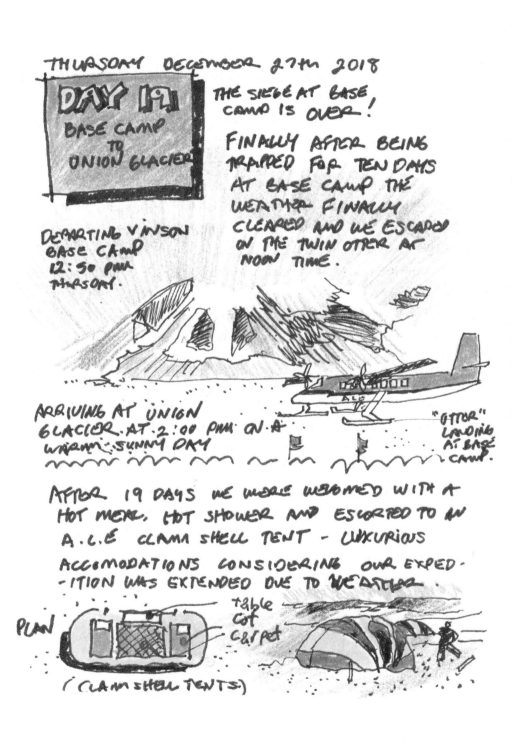

ARRIVING AT UNION GLACIER AT 2:00 PM ON A WARM SUNNY DAY

"OTTER" LANDING AT BASE CAMP.

AFTER 19 DAYS WE WERE WELCOMED WITH A HOT MEAL, HOT SHOWER AND ESCORTED TO AN A.L.E CLAM SHELL TENT - LUXURIOUS ACCOMODATIONS CONSIDERING OUR EXPED-ITION WAS EXTENDED DUE TO WEATHER.

PLAN

table
cot
carpet

(CLAM SHELL TENTS)

ing engines climaxed in a deafening roar. The plane accelerated, dusting up a swirl of white in its wake as it took to the air and disappeared over the lip of the plateau into the valley below. Within seconds, it rose and climbed into a blue, cloudless sky. Banking a wide turn, it disappeared behind Penguin Point.

Our dream of steaming showers, clean clothes, and a hot supper served on ceramic plates in a heated mess hall were within reach. It had been weeks since I had experienced the simple comfort of a chair. Union Glacier promised coffee, laughter, and ample electricity. After 18 days, our Base Camp depravation was coming to an end. We heaved our duffels onto sleds, dragged them to the landing strip, and waited. At noon, the Otter roared in again, spun around, and cut its engines. Shouting farewells to our camp mates, Chris, Mike, Guntis, and I loaded our bags into the storage hold behind the pilots' seats and secured the netting. The members of the flight crew were welcome faces. In a few minutes, the flaps went down. The plane was airborne. Below stretched the no man's land of mountains, glaciers, and crevasses that had astonished me when I first arrived. Mount Vinson slipped into the distance and disappeared behind us.

Ahead lay cold beer, warm conversations, and news of the world, distributed throughout Union Glacier Camp on a fax sheet newspaper. I could run my Antarctica marathon there, solo, doing laps around the runway while I waited for the Ilyushin to arrive and carry us back to Chile. I would forever be the winner and current record holder of the Inaugural Hopecam Antarctic Marathon!

In two days, the lights of the Chilean coast would be in my sight, and I would be surrounded again by trees and cars and concrete buildings with glass windows. At the Shackleton Bar, a converted manor house where explorer Ernest Shackleton returned after rescuing his team from their fraught Antarctic expedition a century earlier, our team would toast his success and ours. Finally, arriving at Dulles International Airport, I would be met with warm embraces and tears from my family who found me circling the baggage claim carousel in search of my bright blue expedition duffels—in time to celebrate the New Year.

Home would not be the same, though. Antarctica had changed me. Mount Vinson had changed me

In our daily lives, we usually try to avoid discomfort. On Vinson, I had embraced it and all the unrelenting wind, bone-chilling cold, endless sunlight, and extreme isolation the continent mustered. I was vulnerable. I was in awe. Over a decade of endurance training had given me the mental strength to face the challenge, but nothing could prepare me for Antarctica's power. Its vast emptiness taught me about the richness of the world I left behind—the world I was now returning to. We expect abundance, I realized. But we rarely honor it. We take small comforts for granted. Huddled in my sleeping bag against the cold, I often wanted nothing more than a chair to sit on. I would never look at these simple comforts the same way again.

Habits don't change without pain or fear, I realized, and Mount Vinson had given me plenty of both. On a brutal and beautiful landscape of ice and stone, that was the cold, hard truth Antarctica taught me.

Images from the Ice

On the opposite and following pages are a few photos from the expedition, some of which you'll recognize from my journal illustrations. As I mentioned earlier in the book, nothing can prepare you for the grand scale and bold beauty of Antarctica. It is a stark but serene palette of white, gray, silver, and blue. I only wish these images could fully convey the experience. To see more (and in color), go to LenForkas.com.

Working the ropes along the slow and arduous trek to reach the peak of Mount Vinson
Not unlike my training a few weeks earlier on Mount Baker, but far more grueling, here I am ascending a daunting 30-degree slope of sheer ice. (Photo courtesy of Chris Warner.)

Mount Vinson Base Camp, elevation 7,021 feet
An ice-block igloo, jokingly called "The Ice Prison," sits among the dispersed tents at our first acclimation point after leaving Union Glacier Camp.

Ascending from Base Camp to Low Camp
Teams travel connected by ropes for safety. We each carried approximately 35 pounds of gear and supplies on our backs while pulling another 80 pounds on sleds.

Opposite page: Low Camp, elevation 9,121 feet
Although we were in Antarctica during 24-hour daylight, simply being in the shadows of the mountains (top photo) sent the temperatures plummeting to minus-40 degrees Fahrenheit. The round lenticular clouds at the mountain peaks (bottom photo) warned us to wait longer to ascend; note the ice blocks around our tents to buffer the winds.

On top of the bottom of the world, Mount Vinson, elevation 16,050 feet
Smiles all around as we celebrate the accomplishment we'd all worked so hard to achieve;
below from left to right: me, Mike, Guntis, and Chris. (Photos courtesy of Andy Cole.)

From desolation to celebration
Above, the view from the Otter plane flying between Base Camp and Union Glacier Camp; below, the dining hut at Union Glacier Camp (left to right: me, Chris, and Guntis).

Making the best of a holiday season away from home
Above, the 37 members of the various teams share the joy of the whitest Christmas ever.
Then after our return to Union Glacier Camp, Mike takes a spin on a fat-tire bike.

It's all about the planes
Everything about the Antarctica experience is made possible by flight. Above is the twin-engine Otter, and below is the huge Ilyushin jet that gets you to and from the continent.

Acknowledgments

This book is the result of a team effort of editors and production talent that brought the story to life. Tim Wendel, an award-winning author and storyteller, and David Frey, managing editor of The Wildlife Society, shaped the rough narrative into a compelling tale that transports the reader to the brutal environment of Antarctica. Andrew Chapman, of Social Motion Publishing, managed the production and formatted more than 50 sketches from my travel notebook for this publication. Thanks to fellow authors Steve Gladis and Lynne Strang for their feedback and encouragement in writing the story.

Thanks to Katie Hanger, owner of Parable Training, who researched and designed a CrossFit training program that produced the strength to haul sleds and shoulder heavy packs on steep ice with confidence. To mountain guide Lyra Pierotly, who taught the use tools and techniques to traverse glaciers and crevasses at Mount Baker, Washington. Thanks to friend Jeff Mascaro, of Smile Mountain Guides, for several days of high-altitude training in the Colorado Rockies weeks before the expedition.

Several climbers on our expedition read the drafts, gave critical feedback, and provided detailed insights into the shared experience during the expedition. Veteran climber Mike Hamill, director of Climbing the Seven Summits, contributed to the story with his insights about leading a group of 12 climbers to the summit. Andy Cole, mountain guide with Adventure Consultants, helped me out of a dangerous situation on the Vinson headwall, and guide Tomas Ceppi kept our team laughing despite the miserable boredom of tent life. Fellow climbers Mrika and Arianit Nikqi, Brad Watts, Glenn Hodges, Kyquan Phong, and Bouchra Baibanou inspired me during the expedition with their personal stories of adventures. Special thanks to Dr. Emily Farkas, who has inspired many of us through her work as a heart surgeon, humanitarian, honorary fellow of World Extreme Medicine, and mountain adventurer. I am grateful for her friendship and encouragement to write this book.

Thanks to teammates and friends Guntis Brands and Mike Paterson whose humor, humility, expertise, and unselfish acts under extreme conditions kept our team safe. Thank you for the feedback on the many drafts of the book.

Thanks to my good friend Chris Warner who gambled by inviting me to join the team. Chris inspired me to take on the challenge, push beyond my limits, and have a lot of fun in the process. His leadership and wisdom made the climb a success and his daily text messages, which are highlighted in this story, were regularly sent home to the living rooms of family and friends during each day of the expedition.

Finally, I would like to thank the children doing battle against cancer who have benefitted from the unique experience that Hope-cam provides. Their stories motivated my team and me to dig deep when times were tough. We climbed a mountain in one of the most inhospitable environments on earth, but it pales in comparison to the challenges these children endure every day fighting for their lives.

About the Author

Len Forkas is the founder and President of Milestone Towers Inc., a Reston, Virginia-based owner and developer of wireless towers in the Mid-Atlantic. Milestone has invested more than $100 million in the development of wireless infrastructure in six states, creating thousands of jobs in construction, engineering, and manufacturing.

In 2014 Len published his first book *What Spins the Wheel: Life and Leadership Lessons from the Race for Hope*. Profits from the sale of the book are donated to support Hopecam's work connecting children with cancer with their friends at school. More than 20,000 copies of the books are in print.

He has appeared on CNN's *Anderson Cooper 360*, Fox News's *Fox and Friends*, Wharton Sirius XM Radio, and the Baltimore/Washington, D.C. affiliates of ABC, Fox, and NBC.

He also serves as Chairman of the Board of Hopecam, the charity he founded in 2003 to use technology to overcome the social isolation of children in treatment for cancer.

For more information on Len, go to LenForkas.com.

Supporting Hopecam

Hopecam has connected over 3,000 children with cancer to 60,000 classmates in 50 states. It has formed partnerships with over 150 hospitals. Seventy percent of Hopecam children attend title-one schools and half are treated at St. Jude's hospital.

All proceeds from this book and Len Forkas's first book support Hopecam's mission.

Hopecam.org

Book Len as a Speaker

Len Forkas has delivered more than 200 speeches, training sessions, and talks, including a TEDx Talk, throughout the United States and numerous countries. From his 20 years' experience as an entrepreneur, philanthropist, author, and endurance athlete, Len will bring the motivation, education, and energy to captivate the audience at your next event. And every dollar of his speaking honorariums fund the mission of the nonprofit, Hopecam.

For video samples and to inquire, go to **LenForkas.com**.

Made in the USA
Middletown, DE
02 October 2023

39929736R00084